THE FLY FISHER'S GUIDE TO CRIMES OF PASSION

Books by Seth Norman

Meanderings of a Fly Fisherman
Flyfisher's Guide to Northern California
The Fly Fisher's Guide to Crimes of Passion

THE FLY FISHER'S GUIDE TO CRIMES OF PASSION

More Sedition from the Master of Meander

Seth Norman

THE LYONS PRESS

Printed in the United States of America

2   4   6   8   10   9   7   5   3   1

Library of Congress Cataloging-in-Publication Data

Norman, Seth.
The fly fisher's guide to crimes of passion : more sedition
from the master of meander / Seth Norman.
p. cm.
ISBN 1-58574-135-3
1. Fly fishing—Anecdotes. 2. Norman, Seth. I. Title.
SH456.N65 2000
799.1'24—dc21
00-57164

To Steve Gore, for fifty years of fine friendship, beginning in 1979.

Contents

Acknowledgments

Writing acknowledgments is a slow job, for all the times I find myself sitting idle, grinning at a memory, occasionally brooding. It's a pleasure and an honor to have a designated moment to give thanks, wink, bow at the waist, fawn a little with great dignity. . . .

First, however, I would like to assert that nearly all those mentioned in Meanderings or Book Two continue to conduct themselves admirably. Take Lisa Jungclas, Enid and Sophia Norman, for example: credited with a couple of words last time around, they have continued to light my life. Sophie has set aside the lovely stonefly nymph outfit Lisa made her for Halloween, the better to pirouette, paint, chase the wretched boys; Lisa gutted out a big life decision or two, and also, remarkably, produced a Max McCloud Norman, in defiance of physiology—or at least a pair of gynecologists who claimed to understand the subject—and with assistance from Drs. Blanchette and Brooks. Max gives Grannie Enid another reason to smile, which she has earned, and deserves, and does rather well. The boyo seems also to entertain his Jungclas ancestors Margaret and Bud—movers extraordinaire, if not yet masters of Swedish—along with Maria Ross and most of the neighbors.

Meanwhile, Eric and Cathy, the Morales twins mentioned within, do thrive; Cathy added Monzos, including son Steven; and older brother Marc drafted Victoria, l'chaim. Eric left here a few hours ago, but I don't see any of them often enough—do you people hear me?

And then . . .

I miss you, Brad Singer. I really do.

Salud, fellow plaintiffs, Steve Bodio, E. Don Thomas, Greg Thomas, John Holt, John Barsness, Web Parton. If it wasn't technically a class-action suit, it was a class act from word one. Thanks to Chuck Watson and Torger Ooas, and most of all to John Kauffman, Esq., who fought the good fight for the right reasons, and triumphed; I think he makes his family proud. For the record, John and Dr. E. Don are just the right guys to draw a man's corpse out of the bar, even if it turns out you don't need a will and autopsy just yet.

To friends near and far-flung, especially the many we leave tomorrow, as today we pack a truck to abandon this Oakland: less to Villa Fairmont staff and clients, after nineteen years, Jim Hess and crew; the Old Eden crowd, Michael Maloney, Mother's Group families Blakeman and Lohser, MidStream patrons Bill and Kate Howe, Angler's Book Supply, Doug's Bugs, Feathercraft, Orvis, the Rumpfs, Sierra Pacific; and to the luminaries who've been kind enough to offer gratis the kind of recognition you can't buy, including Dave Hughes, Lani Waller, Jim Teeny, Andy Puyans, Gerry Darkes. Fishing pals new this time around, Ryzanych, Hickson, Van der Heiden . . . To the Federation of Fly Fishers folks, beginning with Marty Seldon, to CalTrout and Friends of the Trinity . . .

You see how this goes?

So right about now in should step one of the editors we call friends: perhaps Jim Butler or Paul Guernsey, from *Fly Rod & Reel*, where integrity reigns and maintains a sense of humor; or certainly Richard Anderson, of *California Fly Fisher*, who has offered liberty and advice, good food, better books, and his spare bedroom.

And while we're there, here's again credit to others in this industry who inspire and sustain: Nick Lyons, Jim Babb, Jim Pruett, Pete Fromm, Gary LaFontaine and Stan Bradshaw, Dick Wenz, Dave Hughes, Larry Kinney,

Carmen and Nick at Amato, Cool People at Those Other Magazines . . . To Jennifer Lyons at Writer's House. To hosts Thom and Jan Sholseth, in B.C., Sandy and Ponch at the elegant Glacier Bay Country Inn, Gustavus. To Duane Millemen, Host Master . . .

Which leads me to something I think about often:

People provide the great adventures of my life. A few well-chosen make it mean something. People are what I write about, mostly, also my reason for writing. I am a People on my better days, I would argue, and so fairly a player here; but my reflection is hardly the most interesting image, and one of life's great secrets is that narcissism is not merely the cause of most evil, but tedious and banal. With that in mind, I once wrote something about Nick Lyons that I hope is true for me: that he uses the water he fishes as a window into the world, not as a mirror.

Finally . . . years ago I developed, while writing, a sense of what I came to call the "sympathetic mind." You are it. Or I hope so—a reader who keeps company to meanders, and for whom I try to construct stories that reveal the world as I find it.

It sounds odd, I suppose, but writing to me is collaboration, of sorts—a kind of dialogue with the reader. I wouldn't bother if you didn't.

I appreciate that. I wanted to say so, somehow.

I'm sure you know who you are.

THE FLY FISHER'S GUIDE TO CRIMES OF PASSION

1

May Your Face Have Many Wrinkles

Every life should include a few fairy tales, the kind that create smiles that leave your face creased on diagonals—wrinkles so distinctive that later you can spot them in the mirror. "Look! See that crow's-foot? I got that the first time Eric went fly fishing!"

I can say exactly that, as it happens.

Eric's been introducing me as his father or stepfather since he was six years old; now he's twenty-four, a supervisor for SouthWest Airlines. I taught him to spin-fish in 1982, during an era when I traded stocked trout from a local reservoir for the many tubs of laundry detergent required to keep three active children clean. Back then Eric and his twin sister, Cathy, were particularly interested in the gutting process, almost convinced they wanted to see what's inside a fish's eye, though older brother Marc insisted that "Whatever's in there must be gross."

That's context. Add to it this: about a year ago Eric expressed an interest in fly fishing, and started saying, "You know, I think I'd like you to take me."

I looked at him hard with my gimlet eye, which is the left one. "No," I said, "you wouldn't."

"Yes I would," he said indignantly.

"Wouldn't."

"Would so!"

I shook a head heavy with wisdom—encrusted, really. "Eric, I'm afraid that deep in your tiny, hard heart, you believe fly fishing is for old, wrinkled guys."

Eric snorted. "Don't give me that. I'm telling you I want you to take me. Seriously."

I only smiled, thinking *Now you're mine.*

I dogged, delayed, let him build a little steam—no sense making this easy. Sure we would go *someday.* But there was *so* much to learn before we went, etc., etc. What a job it would be. . . .

Then, last month, I jumped him: "It's a four-day expedition, hiking in six miles from ten thousand feet to just about twelve thousand—brutal—looking for golden trout in lakes that just opened for angling this year."

"Sounds great."

"But it will be just after ice-out and way too cold for you."

"I'll be fine."

"You'd only have two weeks to learn to cast—too bad, really."

"When do we start?"

"And you probably can't get all those days off, so maybe next time—"

"*This time, old man.*"

He actually calls me that—O sharper than a serpent's tooth. "Well, let's see. First, tell me this: do you remember all those times you stole my cigarettes, the lovely Winstons you mashed to bits, crushing them in your fingers until their poor broken bodies leaked shreds of precious tobacco while you mumbled some pious mantra the Surgeon General was teaching second graders that year?"

"Yes."

"*Apologize.*"

"Never. Not a chance."

"Oh, all right then."

Marc also wanted to go, but couldn't lose hours from his three jobs, especially the two he works to make payments on his Explorer. Cathy is momming little Stephen; and Big Steve has not yet realized he has wedded fly-fishing opportunity, though he might, once I've had his Raiders habit surgically corrected. All of which meant I could focus on preparing Eric.

The eighty-nine tasks of gearing up: boots, waders, vest, fly box with flies, tippet collection and nippers, sleeping bag and pad, mosquito repellent and sundries. All the explanations: mayflies set sail on the water then rise like souls, caddis have tent wings and fly like moths, for minnows maybe a Muddler and for midges Lint On a Hook. I gave him a piece of clothesline to practice clinch knots.

Also, "Read this book. There will be a test. If you fail the test I will lecture you endlessly, droning on for hours until both of us enter a fugue state, kind of like twilight with no stars, in which all we can do is twitch a little bit—"

"Uh-huh. You just do that."

I sigh. "How I wish I'd spanked you more when I had the chance."

Casting practice. I took him to the Oakland ponds early one afternoon.

"Whatever happens, don't do as I *do*. Do as I *say*. Like this—don't watch me! Tonight you can study Joan Wulff's tape, tomorrow do Mel Krieger's twice and pay attention. Meantime, like this—don't look!"

Eric was the first freshman in Alameda High history to go to the north state finals in both the mile and two-mile, ultimately collecting ten or twelve letters in four sports, so despite my careful tutoring he's soon putting out twenty feet of line, which is all I will allow him. He's doing so well that I reluctantly leave him alone for a few minutes, that he may find a rhythm.

That's when I take a little walk and discover that the Police Activity League has filled the concreted pools on the nearby creek with 800 stocked trout, 794 of which will die of fungal infections within a week. Soon I have Eric stalking them, crouching, kneeling, deftly presenting the tuft of white polypropylene we're using as a practice fly.

He raises half a dozen fish, goes nuts—is still babbling and panting as we return to his truck. "That is *so* cool. Whoa. Incredible."

I figure this is a good time to warn him about smashing graphite in car doors. To emphasize my point I wave about the little faux-rod teaching tool I've made from the top half of an old spinning stick.

The top quarter, more like. Turns out *I'd actually slammed it in the door while climbing into the truck to deliver my warning.* Of course, I desperately try to pretend this accident was deliberate without actually saying so.

"See how easily they break? *See?* This could have been a five-hundred-dollar rod! Let this be a lesson to you!"

"I can't believe you did that."

"What? What? You don't think I . . . ?"

In a nice case of symmetry I send Eric home to practice with the very rod I fished way back when we could still do his math homework together. It's a brilliant move, really. For years Eric has enjoyed telling strangers about the baggy scarlet pants I wore while playing high-competition softball—Pima cotton, the only material that would protect my knees against the bone-deep burns Astroturf inflicts on third basemen. Usually he'll combine this story with another, about the time when he discovered I'd eaten bread mold, which I insisted President Reagan had declared a vegetable, "Specifically, a mature form of relish."

Yeah, man, how that boy goes on. And now, unbeknownst to him, I'd exposed him to a lifetime of a similar humiliation. . . .

Eric, full of natural grace—"Be cool, don't drool," I've wisely advised him—exactly the kind of guy whom Nike hopes to swoosh and whose entrance into a room full of women causes that choked silence created by baited breath—

—*Eric first practiced casting with a gray fiberglass rod bought new for ten dollars.*

Hah! I can't wait until he's tackle savvy enough to be embarrassed by this. I sure hope the pictures turn out.

Departure day arrives. We pile gear into the back of the new Toyota truck Eric bought when I offered him my 1981 model. Such a smart aleck.

At least he brought the right music. "Brought the right music," he says with a sly grin, and we're buying a Stairway to Heaven, which is another item that I suggest "is probably cheaper than this truck."

It's a long drive full of conversation. After a couple of hours I point out the lake where, a decade ago, Cathy got up on water skis her very first try—and stayed up, surprised and grinning for five hundred yards. "That actually can't be done," I tell Eric soberly.

"But she did it," he says proudly.

I know it's true. I was there. And the photos turned out.

By the time we are heading north through the mountains long shadows lean east across the road. It's clear we won't reach the trailhead until after midnight. Which means, of course, we should really fish now, then hope to set up camp before three A.M.

I remember a stream not far from this highway, one I last visited as a blushing boy of thirty. It's about a half cast across, winding through marshy scrub brush that might be called bracken.

"Little tiny trout," I tell Eric. "Wild, and very beautiful."

He's all for it.

When to help, when to leave be. Balance. Perspective. A mistake of my father's taught both of us not to push things. And long ago, Eric taught me a corollary to that rule. As with some true stories this one works rather too well—is so apt and instructive I've never dared write it down. The illustrated version in stereo is too long, so suffice this:

Cub Scouts have a project called the Pine Box Derby. Each cubber with a parent "as guide" is to create a car from a block of wood, four plastic wheels, and four finishing-nail "axles." Eric and I gnawed the edges of ours using a Buck knife, most of a hacksaw blade, and two grades of sandpaper. Eric actually did sand one side concave, and while the asymmetric result pleased him no end I endeavored to carve a balance with his hand resting on the back of mine.

I looked too intent. He started laughing.

"What?"

"Well. You know, it's just a *little* car. It's for fun. It's not so *serious*."

By God, he was right. So I let it go the way he liked it, answering his question of "What kind is it?" as best I could. "It's a bent Studebaker." Then, in jest, I suggested we might consider furniture polish rather than paint—an idea Eric seized.

At the troop meeting the cars were judged first on appearance. Such cars: a fantastically detailed 1/64-scale version of a Porsche; sliver cars with molded lead weights embedded into slots countersunk above the wheels; cars that were literally primed, painted and Simonized. With flame decals. With pin stripes. Cars no seven-year-old had ever touched.

Eric looked confused. Several of his den mates looked disdainful. "What's *that*, Eric?"

"A bent Studebaker."

"What?"

"They're *famous*."

"But you didn't even paint it."

"It's got *Pledge*," he insisted.

I wanted to slap myself hard.

The Porsche won for looks. Then came the race, heats of eight cars running on a sloping wood track. Forget winning; I just hoped the Studebaker's wheels would stay on, and that our poor pine box would at least roll to the finish line while my own cub was still young. But an undaunted and conspicuously hopeful Eric stationed himself at the bottom of the ramp, ready to cheer, while I crouched twenty feet away framing him in the viewfinder of a 110 camera.

I was still framing when the starter signaled and released the cars for their two-second run, so it was through
that plastic eye that I saw and snapped this image of Eric,
his hands thrown way up in the air, dark eyes wide as
plums, staring right at me in delight and disbelief.

He won.

He won the next heat.

And the next, I think, but don't ask me how. Eventually he came in third out of a whole bunch of cars, placing
just after two of the Simonized, lead-slung slivers. (Later
the first-place father baldly acknowledged he'd built his
car years before, for this son's older brother. This confes-
sion prompted the second-place father to snort, "Hell, at
least I let my kid sand mine a little." No kidding.)

Eric said, "Boy, was that great," by which, I decided,
he meant something important.

Of course I did not think about all that as Eric and I strung
rods, or as we approached the little stream. I was busy selecting a Humpy for him to tie on—a dry that would let
him see the effects of drag on drift. "Now," I said. "You
want to go over everything and learn a little bit, or have at
it yourself in a wild, haphazard way?"

"I'd really like to have at it."

Damn. "Go to it."

In the next half-hour I caught several small rainbows
while trying to watch Eric only with my peripheral vision.
He caught bracken, of course, hooked his rod tip, a willow and several guides—all at once. But he seemed
patient, and he did approach the stream like Hiawatha
edging up on a deer, crouching lower than my knees will
let me without kneeling, and using every tiny bit of shrub
as cover.

He was stooped behind one of these when I heard him
hiss "Something bit it!"

"Great," I called back indulgently, remaining twenty yards away in order to more obviously mind my own business. "Good work!"

Cast, cast. The sun was well down now. Pretty evening, twilight with stars.

"Got him!"

What?

"I got him."

"Great!" I could tell by the bend in his rod he had either a snag or a small trout wrapped in big weeds. Just then this *thing* started churning water near his feet, a green-backed animal with a broad yellow belly. . . .

"Eric—"

"I got him!"

And when the brown was in his hands—a male as long as my forearm from wrist to elbow with a kipe like a snarling German shepherd—Eric looked up at me.

I remembered. So many years later but I could have been peering through a cheap 110 lens, seeing this expression full of life and faith, disbelief mixed, inexplicably, with a nearly visible certainty that life holds this kind of pleasure for people who know "it's for fun," who will thrill to polish a little car with Pledge. And I understood in that instant again, if not quite in the words I'd find later, that learning to fish flies ain't no *task*, campers, however complicated, difficult or demanding; and that even if you do learn well and only enjoy using the most expensive tackle at million-dollar lodges, it's *still* about the feeling Eric showed on his face.

Fourteen, perhaps fifteen inches, was Eric's first fish on a fly, a dry—first time out—from a stream that can't have many trout that size. We described it for hours. Laughing. Shaking our heads and moaning and retelling the story until it felt positively legendary, a chapter from Beowulff, *at least*.

Fairy tales ... a few, I think life should have, carving crow's-feet beside our eyes. I think Eric left this one between Cathy's ski miracle mark and another Marc gave me first time he taught a class at the Boy's Club. These each have a home near creases left by friends named Steve, across from the Enid Crevasses, above Sophie Canyon, west of Max draw and Lisa's divide—

Blessed wrinkles.

May your face have many.

2

Wha's Up?

Anticipation is such a pleasurable part of fly fishing that it sometimes seems a shame to go out someplace, cast, and try to catch something. Whenever I daydream a trip the weather is balmy and the air full of hatches exactly matched by the patterns I'm carrying. Sly brown trout the size of basset hounds hurl themselves at my flies, then fight like demons; the stream is wholly mine, unless I want a nude sunbather, maybe two; I never have to tie knots. Food just happens, periodically, during days in which I get 27 hours of sunlight, 22 of which are dusk and dawn.

In real life it's not like that *every* time. I mean, once there were, like, *three* nude sunbathers.

It's the end of March, the first time I can get away for more than a day since November; so of course the snow level falls to two thousand feet. I try reaching a little lake twelve hundred feet higher than that, on a five-hour drive spent mostly thinking about Brad, a friend I've had for thirty-two years, now dead at forty-six; and at 2:30 A.M., exactly one mile from the cabin, I begin to slide backwards on an icy incline in the new-to-us van I just paid for, descending with spinning wheels toward a bridge.

"*Wha's up?*" I say aloud, which startles me.

It may interest you to learn that there are trends in last words, according to Steve Gore, my private-investigator friend. At least there were in Oakland, the years he worked for the Alameda County Public Defender's Office.

"Two victims last month, both drug dealers shot with witnesses present, were each killed right after saying 'Wha's up?' "

" 'Wha's up?' Why is that?"

"No idea. But the same thing has happened to a couple others I know about."

So wha's up with saying "Wha's up?" at 2:30 A.M.?

I must have filed away the phrase for use in dire straits, when it could be all over. But when *I* say it, the van stops sliding. Less suspicious people might suggest the cessation of movement had something to do with letting off the accelerator.

In any case I'm left in freezing limbo on the slope of a remote dirt road late at night when I'm tired to the bone. It's too steep to sleep here; also, I can't get over to the side of the road—which is a ditch anyway—and while I don't expect any cars out here until morning, if any did happen along our molecules would merge. Then there's the matter of the fishing I'll miss. . . .

It starts to snow harder.

Note at this juncture: *nothing like this happens in my daydreams*. Fear, or at least alarm, never bothers me for an instant; I am never cold, weary, baffled. And where's the food?

"Hell, I'll throw the chains in with the deal," the van seller had said. "Case you go to Tahoe."

There they are. Two chains and a chain tensioner.

One chain tensioner. *Uno,* as we said in Arizona. In Malay, *satu*—I could go on, but perhaps you recall that one is the loneliest number.

"Well well well," I say. "Well."

Then . . .

I put on one chain, with tensioner. I put on the other chain, which clearly needs a tensioner.

We are not happy. The Cosmic Mind and I have a discussion; it does not appear to resent my expressive language. Nor is it impressed, apparently. Then it asks me a question using the Royal Plural: Are We not the manufacturer of a fine coil lanyard for staffs, pliers, nets and other landing devices? And do We not have several of these in Our tackle?

Why, yes, Cosmic, We do.

They don't *just* work. Oh, no. They work so well as a chain tensioner that I'm cackling as I churn through the icy mire that last mile, proffering congratulations all round, promising to take product shots of two stretched-straight lanyards holding fast.

We are too cool to drool, it's a fact. Soon the cabin is warm and I fall asleep not caring one whit if I'm snowed in or not.

I'm snowed in, probably, I see in the morning. I still don't care, but the ice everywhere gives me pause, as does a surety that the lake's temperature will be too chilly to take with any finger I hope to enjoy wearing the rest of the day. Also, there's this small matter of a twenty-knot wind.

It doesn't seem fair, to be both cold and windy. Then again, I was a cad in my youth, when I had the chance, as I recall while drinking instant coffee without cream, which is how Brad drank his joe, about a dozen cups a day.

"I was a cad with Brad." He'd have liked that nonsense rhyme. For thirty-two years we had little in common, save for a sense of play and great affection. We chased women together in high school, and Lord, he did love the dim ones. He once convinced a date that my skin was a different color *from the waist down*. No, I mean he *convinced* her.

Brad was tall and lanky and by his sophomore year could grow a full beard or sideburns over a three-day weekend. His father owned a bar in downtown Phoenix, Bud's House of Doubles, on First and Adams. When we were fifteen or sixteen we spent hot summer nights there, dancing with the go-go girls—we weren't studs, but kind of like pets—and playing pool on the pay table by slipping a matchbook cover into the coin mechanism. My heart broke there one night, watching an old prostitute train a girl no older than I. Bud's was the first place I went to where I knew people carried guns.

Brad wouldn't talk about his parents' divorce, but when he was old enough to drive we would sometimes leave town in his Cougar to spend three or four days in Vegas with his father, now a pit boss at the Vegas Club, and his father's new wife, a cocktail waitress at the Mint. (For the life of me, I can't remember why my parents let me do this.) I remember Brad's silence during those journeys, the hours he was lost to thought or mourning. It was no use and no help to prod him to talk, but he somehow made me understand it was important for me to just *be* there, riding shotgun as he drove a bleak road.

That was a little bit of it. These were defining years, a time when I think each of us believed we were cutting ourselves from whole cloth. All these big firsts, work, sex, a little violence and lots of realizations—right and wrong—about the life coming our way. Brad was probably the first friend I knew as more or less an adult, who knew me as well; and whom I appreciated vastly while understanding how different we were. Senior year, for example, I buckled down in school for the first time ever, because I would need a scholarship. Meanwhile, Brad dropped out to do the only thing he ever wanted to do, sell records. Then, while the rest of us diddled in college, he set to making himself a retail music and publishing mogul, a multi-millionaire who came out with his son to ramble about in Viola, my '78 Toyota RV, and to fish—all three of us—in an eight-foot, four-inch pram adapted from the shell of an old sailboat.

About once a week, I think about him. Same as when he was alive. Only before I would smile, occasionally call.

Because of the wind, I leave the float tube in the van, opting instead for some high rubber boots I packed mostly by chance. I will fish the face of the small dam. I know there's a drop-off about twenty-five feet out, and that if I can hang a nymph right there, six to eight feet down from an indicator, I'll have a chance to intercept cruisers. In light as low as is left beneath churning gray clouds, the fish may even come up the ledge, hunting nearly to my feet.

Throwing a 4-weight line with a yarn indicator tied eight feet up from a nymph into the teeth of a twenty-knot wind with marginal room for a backcast is a dicey operation. It's best to think of the yarn as your fly, I've found; and it was the yarn I needed to land thirty or forty feet out, so the nymph could sink before it blew back to fish hanging along the edge. It helps to spend some time pulling the fly line straight. Cold coils won't cast, it's true; and it's probably as important to stretch your own tendons and muscles, warm the joints. These days my right shoulder crackles audibly, with a sound very much like Rice Krispies when you pour on the milk.

It ain't an elegant game, but I confess that I enjoy watching the indicator bob with the wind, imagining that motion twitching the out-of-sight nymph. It's difficult to keep the line anywhere close to tight; but when the yarn takes a dive I set up on a rainbow of eight inches, a wild creature with a large eye in a tiny head. Just as I kneel to land him, the sun fractures a cloud bank, and for an instant the gray pine wall along the opposite bank is pierced through by splinters of platinum light which break into brilliant bits on the water, are driven by wind, and seem even to have sound—a crackling, of course.

"That is a *dazzle* of light," I think, and send the little fish back to his own.

The next fish is a big stocker with a kipe and attitude. His ferocity fools me: I tweak the hook from his jaw without touching him, presuming he needs no help reviving.

Wrong. I see him drift down, struggle to stabilize, turn on one side. He's still near enough: I wade almost to the top of my rubber boots, then rake him toward me with the rod, using it just as the manufacturer recommends. The stocker resents this. I insist. He rights himself indignantly. I let him rest a little, watch, then annoy him some more, until he slams his tail with such violence I am splashed up to the knee.

But do they ever write? Just a casual note: "Doing fine, thanks, eating mostly caddis," or, "Despite you, Sadist, I spawned."

Two other anglers drive up, chat a little—yes, the road is now passable, at least with four wheel drive. They launch tubes. One fishes a midge dry, misses a few hits, hooks one. The other catches a couple on a brown Woolly Bugger. I land another small fish, break off a bigger one, then hit two small wilds and one heavy stocker on a fat copper-ribbed nymph. The Bugger guy hits a big one.

And like that, through the morning. About noon I head back to the cabin for breakfast. A friend and his pal show up to chat for an hour. Eventually, I head back to the lake with my own tube. The pair of anglers is whacking them hard at the inlet, on dragonfly nymphs, but the afternoon is as cold as the morning, and it only warms to start snowing. They worry about the road and head out. Immediately thereafter I take four big fish, then notice that the skin on my hands has dried and begun to fissure a little. My feet, at least, have had the good sense to go numb.

The wind dies down and now it's snowing harder, big flakes brushing up against each other, whispering as they meet the lake, creating images and sound so excited I stop fishing to watch and listen—so much movement, so gentle, completely encompassing. For a moment I think that soon I won't be able to see the far shore, but there is nothing frightening about that. I am trembling for other reasons when suddenly the sun breaks through again, light angling from low in the western sky this time, shining from beneath the dark cloud bank right above me. A billion flakes are illuminated from below; they glow faintly gold. There is red in the air, and a color that looks rust against the winter-bare branches of deciduous trees, more a brass on the evergreen limbs, then gold again everywhere. It is all so lovely I catch my breath, and what I feel makes me remember that Brad is dead.

Sometimes it just happens that way.

I am so cold by the time I reach the cabin that I am staggering and the air inside burns my hands, so cold I clumsily fill the tub with water that feels fine on my face but scalds my feet. It is twenty minutes before I stop shaking. I make a little food, pour myself two fingers, sit still for a while thinking about Brad, then dial the radio to a country-western station and start tying a variation of the Assam dragon. It evolves one step at a time, until I find a combination I really like a lot. It's an Assam, mostly, built around a glass bead, so that when you hold it to the light it looks to have a heart of gold.

For once, I am able to tie the same pattern over and over.

The next day I take between twelve and fifteen fish in less than two hours, casting my dragon from shore while waiting for the wind to die down enough to launch my tube. It never does.

The day after that I drop down into the valley. In the afternoon I fish the Lower Sac. The wind is still blowing, hard enough to chill the blanket caddis. I busy myself with a couple of tools I am testing, prototypes that are attached to my vest in various ways. Incredibly, a passing angler recognizes me. I ask him how. He says, "I think it was all that stuff hanging off you that did it."

I laugh then, and laugh more later, when I meet a pal and tell him the story. We catch a few fish—he gets a twenty-incher, and late in the evening when the wind dies down a little I wade a flat I'd never explored, liking it a lot. We visit another pal for dinner, eat great spaghetti, drink way too much red wine, laugh until late. I spend the night in Redding with the friend who lives there, and the next morning ramble around looking at country, enjoying the company best of all.

That afternoon I head to a small bass lake I've heard good things about. It's in a pasture, turns out. That's a problem, because all the drive over I've been watching usually vertical objects bowing to the wind. Even so, I am unprepared for the blast that catches the van door when I open it eight inches—thirty miles an hour, I bet, and the water on the downwind side of the lake actually looks like it's piled up higher than on the other side.

I can't fly fish in this, I think. Then I wonder, Well, what *can* I do?

Keep fully fifty feet of intermediate fly line sailing in the air indefinitely, for one thing, just by rolling it out and raising my rod. If I lay the tip down fast I can "dap" at long range.

It's a whole bunch of fun, sort of. I take two little bass, then one of about a pound, before deciding to drive on to another lake on the way home. I figure that by the time I arrive, the wind will die down, as it did late the evening before.

It doesn't, though. Instead, it only turns much colder.

I decide to prowl a dike into the dark anyway. It is a different kind of dusk: no rain, no glow, only the blowing wind and all sorts of blue and gray light. I watch a beaver swimming against the chop as it crosses a cove. I see the wakes of three large fish move away from cover in a shallow arm of the lake where water must have warmed a little, but can't get close to them. That's all right: it's so cold, so windy that the evening has a crazy feel to it, wild in a way that I like. I fling casts downwind, but the rod is so blown about—whipped and wobbled—that I don't actually grasp that I've hooked a fish until it jumps. Even then I can't believe it.

I'm still stunned when I land him. Got to be three pounds. Or two and a half.

It's enough. I just watch the world for a little while, then drive.

"How was your trip?"

"Good."

"What'd you do?"

"Fished. Thought about Brad."

"That's all?"

"More or less."

Lisa cocks her head at me. "You're too quiet," she says. "What's up?"

A trip's never the way I daydream it, if you must know the truth. Which is just one of the reasons I always go again.

3

Hail the Humpy King

On the sixth day we were chased by maniacal she-sea lions. Never mind that—it was the afternoon before when I had one of those defining moments in life, a sea change of self-image coincident with a high tide that pushed up the estuary into the stream mouth, passing on its way a flock of glutted seagulls and an obese brown bear.

We rode the rising water in our two inflatables, motoring through the first staging pool to anchor in a channel just above. Captain Dan Foley maneuvered our craft into position, following the directions of Brian O'Keefe, photographer extraordinaire and secret gymnast. Guidemaster Rich Culver and Dr. Aric Ludvig were stationed just below us, first mate John "Rocky" Rock at the engine.

For an hour O'Keefe laid out long casts with a floating line while I hurled a hi-density shooting head, a "Head Chopper." Brian's more elegant efforts stuck two fish. I hooked up about every other cast, landing half a dozen.

Only this: Brian's salmon were chrome aerialists, fierce, fresh cohos of fifteen pounds—the prize for which we'd come. My beasts, on the other hand, were the distant, disdained cousins of that species, humpbacks—AKA "humpies" or "pinks"—a species half the size of silvers and less than svelte, with bodies grotesquely distorted by ripening hormones. Humpies spawn every autumn, but run en masse during even-numbered years, when they become anathema to serious Alaska anglers, a scourge.

Slam—another one. This buck drove through the shallows, his hugely swollen shoulders cresting a riffle. He found a deeper pocket, dove down—then came up to leap three times, finally reversing direction in midair.

"Again?" said Captain Dan. "Man, you just can't keep them off you."

"They're everywhere," Culver shouted unhappily. He was bent over and stripping fly line, intent as a heron. Rich has incredible eyes, but even he can't always slip his fly away from a humpy attack, and two days before had broken a 500-dollar rod trying to rip free from one.

My pink went up again, turning sideways as he ascended, then double-slapping the surface with his tail as he fell. The next moment he caught the current and convinced the reel's drag to sing sixteenth notes.

"You do hang a lot of those," Brian said sympathetically. "Maybe you should try this side."

I nodded, saying nothing as the fish edged in, dogging every inch and snapping his head from side to side. His jaws gaped as he struggled; flesh had shrunk away from his gums, exposing long canines. Suddenly he saw the boat and spooked: if his fangs were a wolf's, his attitude was still strictly pit bull. I felt his final run strain the rod shaft right through the cork rings.

When at last I tailed him, I found he'd fought the fly with equal vigor, gnawing hair from the wing and cutting loose a silver-tinsel rib. I slipped the streamer from his kipe, pointed his nose upstream, then gave him half a minute to recover his senses. I might have saluted, secretly, as I completed the release. *May your milt meet many eggs.*

Ninety seconds later, six feet into a swing through the channel, I set the hook once more, setting off another explosion.

"They are such a pain!" cried Culver.

"Really," murmured Brian. "Why don't you try my side for a while?"

That's when it happened. Maybe it took a moment, or time enough for this new buck to race his own roostertail for thirty yards, pause, speed part way back, then drive down with slugs of his tail strong enough to cramp my hands:

Please, no, I thought, impaled on an insight, utterly exposed to myself, deep down, where viscera twisted into a clinch knot of understanding. And though the realization was ugly indeed, at least there was security in knowing my wretched self so well. Perhaps that's why I let the outer edges of a smile almost reach my ears.

"Gentlemen," I said slowly, speaking loudly enough for both boats. "Gentlemen, I had hoped to keep this from you . . . but that would be wrong. So you may as well know—" with a grand gesture I pointed out toward my surging humpy, which leaped right on cue— "that I love these squat sons-of-bitches. I just love them."

A silence, then Rich snorted. "You are kidding, aren't you?"

"Not only that," I continued quickly, "if fresh humpies like these aren't fun to catch—wild things clear through their hearts—then I'm not the most satisfied man on this stream."

"I don't think he is," said Dr. Aric.

"I am," I vowed. "Satisfied. Really."

"Kidding, I meant."

"Save your pity, I tell you."

"He must be kidding," insisted Rocky.

"I am not. All I'm saying is—" I had to think a second, and to muster my defiance "—*that I am the Humpy King.*"

It had been a long haul to reach my misty domain, beginning two weeks before, late in the evening of an August day I'd spent roasting on a boat in the Sacramento Delta. The sky there was the white of dirty steam, and the water looked like a blend of coffee and algae only because you can't actually see the PCBs, dioxin, heavy metals and pesticide residues. I'd roused only once all afternoon, to grunt appreciation when a sly radio announcer said, "Okey doke, folks, Stockton's experiencing a cooling trend: it's dropped a degree, to one hundred and four." In a burst of optimism, I hoped that summer days spent in California's Central Valley count as time served in Purgatory; then I worried that they might be some kind of ominous preparation. Hard to know. Either way, while driving home to Oakland I noticed that the heat waves shimmering above the freeway were too washed out and weak to create a convincing mirage.

The promise of cool relief came from a message Rich Culver had recorded on my answering machine. "Come up. Come up if you can. We're talking about exploration really, sailing a mother ship south from a lodge in Gustavus to places where Alaska Fish and Game hasn't even done a census yet. It's a gamble, but you're welcome along. Give me a call."

Rich and I had met two years before, while he was doing a slide presentation on southeastern Alaska, his new home. I sat mesmerized as he showed shot after shot of small rivers tumbling down timbered mountains to fjords, along with photos of silver salmon and steelhead framed by backdrops of cedars and spruce. "This isn't the Alaska most people know," he said, "it's not Bristol Bay or any-place else fly fishers usually visit. But it's probably Alaska the way you dreamed it would be: full of fish, bears, and eagles, empty of people. When I got there I just couldn't believe it."

That was saying something. For many years Rich had been one of California's more devoted steelhead bums, when not guiding at Clearwater House. Then, at the invi-tation of a client, Dr. Aric Ludvig, Rich visited Juneau. As the legend is now told, he'd loped in to Aric's emergency room, spied a nurse named Harriet and, almost instantly, tied his half of a blood knot that now has two droppers, Misha and Lynzey.

Rich's young family, it turned out, would be of conse-quence to mine. "Absolutely, bring them," he insisted, when I called back to relay Lisa's conditions for my re-lease. "Bring her and the baby. We'll put them up at the Country Inn in Gustavus for a couple of days—they'll love it. Then they can fly back to Juneau to stay with Harriet and the girls. Believe me, they will party."

That's how Sophie, eighteen months old and the length of my best brown trout, came to be standing on the seat of an Alaska Airline 727 nine days later, employing for deplan-ing tourists that cupped hand wave of Queen Elizabeth's while cooing "Bye-see-ya-bye-bye." For the smiles that she produced she could have been spraying nitrous oxide.

I wasn't smiling soon after: somewhere in the off-loading process our Minolta disappeared forever, and my rods had apparently jumped plane during our Seattle stopover. But my mood was positively sanguine compared to that of the woman ahead of me at the Alaska Airlines service counter: "That's all my clothing you've lost, every-thing for this trip."

The agent looked her up and down. "Listen," she said. "You're about my size: I've got plenty of clothes. We'll get you by, I promise. And you'll love Gustavus."

That was such a nice personal touch that I asked her how she was fixed for 6-weight fly rods.

Both the Glacier Bay Country Inn and its sister, Whalesong Lodge, run vans to the Gustavus airport. While waiting for ours I noticed a face familiar to me from fishing trade shows. I nudged Lisa. "I think that's Brian O'Keefe. The famous photographer. I don't know—he looks dubious to me. Probably a rake."

"Him? Oh, he does not. He looks very nice."

He did seem so at introductions. Three minutes later he was insisting that the van driver, a fetching woman, closely examine his "fly-fishing muscle."

"No really," he insisted. "You've got to see this."

I don't want to talk about what he did after that. I did learn the key to the driver's tolerance, however, a few miles down the road, as she spoke to Lisa about Alaska's famously unbalanced ratio of men to women. "Oh, it's true," she observed wryly. "But what smart girls here will tell you is this: 'The odds are good, but the goods are odd.' Believe it."

Rich was waiting for us when we pulled into the driveway, near where the main lodge nestled among pines before a meadow blazing with fireweed. We hauled gear straight up to one of the cabins clustered on a slope. I think I ex-pected something dark—a trapper's shack redecorated once since the Klondike era. Instead, ours was large and light, paneled in pale woods, immaculately clean. For Sophie they'd brought in a lovely white crib with a tiny cov-erlet. Lisa was won over.

Sure enough, at the main lodge, a structure of many gables on the elegant side of rustic, we met owners Ponch and Sandy Marchbanks, then their grandson, Kenny, a month older than Sophie. Immediately I suspected that it was Kenny who ordered the crib. I know he took one look at my daughter and it was a Luv thing.

More introductions followed at dinner, where we sat at a long table in front of a wall of windows. Beyond these was a grassy airstrip that local wildlife, including moose and a black-bear family, have adopted as a playground. I don't know what that does for landings, but it can make for excellent dinner theater.

Not that I had attention to spare. In a lifetime of eat-ing banal American, with one year's digressions for mar-ginal Malaysian and rural Chinese, another for Middle Eastern cuisine, I'd regularly encountered meals like this only at the Bay Wolf Café in Oakland, one of the finest restaurants in an area known for the West Coast's best. True, I was washing dishes there at the time, but they fed me twice a shift.

"This is that good," I whispered to Lisa after the salmon ravioli appetizer, and again during the entree of Dungeness Crab. Both times Lisa only nodded because, unlike me, she won't hiss with her mouth full.

Ultimately, chef Jon Emanuel slipped out of the kitchen long enough to see that we were satisfied. Just as I thought—a San Francisco Culinary Institute grad. Ponch himself followed soon after, to tell stories in a voice that should convince CNN to finally replace James Earl Jones. Sandy, in turn, has one of those soft Southern accents full of smiles. Which is deceptive: she keeps cockatoos with beaks like pruning shears, and the next morning she whacked two yearling bears off the porch with a broom. "Well, it was for their own good, don't you know?" she insisted sweetly. "I mean, should they be rough-housing out there like that? I don't think so."

Soon after the bear-rout we four anglers loaded onto one of the inn's own sportfishing boats for a quick run up the Icy Straits, headed toward one of the creeks feeding Bartlett Cove. Clear and quick, the stream looked much like one of the Sierra freestoners where I would expect native rainbows and the occasional wild brown.

None of which would ever reach the size of the salmon soon slashing its way across riffles, then rifling into the air in a leap easily as high as Rich's body when erect—which he wasn't, surrendering to the pressure the hooked fish exerted. This coho, or maybe it was the next one, ran Rich clear out into the estuary, ripping out backing as the 8-weight rod did isometrics. By then Rich was yelping with excitement. And relief: by that point he hadn't caught a fish in almost twelve hours, and to call Rich simply "fanatic" is like suggesting Mike Tyson is merely a boor with women, and awkward in crowds. While Brian O'Keefe popped out his cameras, the doctor and I headed upstream.

Within minutes Aric was tied to eager silver, and I to a fish unlike any I'd ever seen before. About two pounds, it had colors of such subtlety that I decided it might be the prettiest trout I'd ever seen—which it wasn't technically, but a char, my first sea-run Dolly Varden. I studied it carefully, to fix the image forever.

Eventually, I traipsed upstream after Aric. I caught up to him at a spot where a submerged gravel bar split a pool down the center, creating on the far side a backwater eddy, and on the near a moderate run. Aric had already busted off a pair of silvers in the current side of the seam; I soon lost one on a leap. But we saw enough boils to convince us that an entire school of fish was resting along the quiet bank opposite, just out of reach.

We crossed at the riffle upstream and edged out along the bar. Aric, now throwing a hot-orange streamer, drifted it along the seam's softer side. A silver took there, spilled into the current, then shot out of the water like a javelin.

"Like a steelhead," I said.

"Exactly," shouted Aric.

While the two of them danced I rolled out my own fly, an Egg Sucking Leech tied out of marabou and from a pattern I'd found in a book. It swam slowly across the current before sliding into a shadow cast by quicker water, where it suddenly turned black and twenty-five inches long with chrome flanks, a black tail, and a turbocharger.

"SSSSSssssttt," said the line.

It was a borrowed Scott 9-weight I was using, one of the stiffer prototypes Richard had brought along. I'd been delighted with the way it slung heavy line, but the second time the fish and I struck each other the multimillion-modulus graphite flexed clear down to the stripping guide.

Six leaps, I counted, but I may have missed one. The fish managed an eighty-foot run in a sixty-foot pool by racing half a circle, dragging the line in an arc behind him. Soon it became one of those battles that leave your forearm swollen, stinging with lactic acid build-up.

Each of the four fish I took in the next two hours was just as brutal. Aric caught even more; by the time we waded back down to the boat our hands were so tight with strain we looked like men wearing claws. Rich failed to notice, however, and chastised us severely. "You should have been here," he insisted. "I mean, it's just been great."

Sailing back up the bay, Captain Jim asked if we'd mind stopping a few minutes, to collect one of the region's other mighty fish, the halibut. I watched O'Keefe, who only fishes about 349 days a year, roll his eyes. "Uh-oh. Big flatties. Barn-doors. Lots of work."

The boat's three rods were the length and stiffness of broomsticks and we baited the 9/0 hooks with fish fillets each big enough for dinner. Brian was tending one of these rigs when I saw the tip-top nod.

He squinted an instant, then said, "Gee. Dr. Aric, would you mind holding this for a moment? Believe I need a cup of hot chocolate."

"Sure," said the doctor, whose nature, I would find, was relentlessly good.

"Thanks so much."

Brian slipped into the galley. The rod nodded again.

"Brian!" Aric called, "You've got a bite!"

"Oh my," answered Brian airily. "Can you take that for me?" He was already sitting down.

"But—"

If such strikes made sound, this one would have thumped like a mattress dropped from a third-story window. Five minutes later, while Aric was still grunting and lifting and staggering around the stern with teeth locked and his back making faint cracking sounds, I joined Brian on the couch.

"You knew," I said accusingly.

"Moi? Surely you don't believe that?"

And if smiles made noise, Brian's would cackle.

Eighty pounds, that monster. Imagine this: two days before this, three guys had caught a bigger one right off the Gustavus pier. Bigger, as in five times that size—400 pounds plus.

We returned to Gustavus nearly at dusk, to transfer our gear directly onto the *Steller*, the seventy-foot mother boat where we'd spend the next five days. It was an impressive introduction: A huge boom lifted our inflatables from dock to rear deck as if they were seashells. We stopped back at the inn for a superb dinner, then I said farewell to Lisa as she made plans to watch whales and visit glaciers, and to Sophie as she gurgled queries to Kenny about his prospects.

I'm pretty sure both my ladies noticed me leave.

It was dark when Captain Dan Foley showed us around his ship. Originally built as a research vessel for Alaska Fish and Game, the *Steller* was named for German naturalist Georg Wilhelm Steller, who in 1741 accompanied Vitus Bering on a voyage of exploration for imperial Russia. That's appropriate enough, as Foley now custom-charters ecologically interesting voyages for anglers, kayakers, and those interested in expeditions well off any path ever beaten. There's room: the *Steller* is enormous in a manageable-feeling way, with three decks, a vast open stern, warm galley, shower, laundry, laboratory, and four sleeping quarters. The eighteen-foot-wide pilot house has three walls of windows and stands high enough above the water to offer a commanding view of life—or species thereof, which may be identified using Dan's library of field identification guides. I was mesmerized by the computer screens on which run navigational programs, with graphics so exciting I almost reached for a quarter.

Our own bunkroom, we found, had teak paneling, plush carpet, and the soft lighting of my favorite bar. There was even a table with booth seating; there we broke out a bottle of Aric's brandy even as we smeared on a seasickness potion the doctor's pharmacist had cooked up. I asked Aric to examine two small bites I'd suffered while fishing. What had been bloody little pits were now beginning to swell.

"Whitesock bites!" said Aric happily. "Whoa. The really cool thing is that they don't actually sting you, or suck blood through a tube like mosquitoes. Instead, they chew a small hole, really ragged and nasty. Sometimes the infections that set in are just spectacular. Really, they are."

Really cool? *Relentless*, this good nature of his. Later, as the whole back of my hand began to inflate, I wondered if both of our conditions could be surgically corrected.

That night, while the *Steller* churned through mists and past the starlit silhouettes of coastal mountains, we better acquainted ourselves with Captain Dan and the crew. Dan is a long Maine man with a visage slightly sterner than Ahab's and a laugh that shakes doors. Twenty years ago, he'd migrated to Juneau for a job that soon went south; so he and two pals built a Grand Banks dory and rowed it to Gustavus. What Dan found there sent him back all the way to Maine to buy a lobster boat, build a trailer to haul it across the country, then sail back to Gustavus, there to single-handedly kick-start the local crab trade. Now he lives in the only house on his own road, Dungeness Lane, a name he chose "because UPS needed an address to deliver to, and because crab money built what's out there."

Kathy Leary, our chef magnifique, also cooks at the Glacier Bay Country Inn, when she isn't working as Gustavus's administrative librarian or momming for four. She's the warm sort of woman who makes you want to catch a cold so she'll feed you all day, pile on the blankets, maybe read you a story. Of course, O'Keefe had to show her his fly-fishing muscle. Later he took her dancing in the galley—imagine jitterbugging in a closet—and thereafter did pot duty without a whimper.

John Rock, "Rocky," turned out to be not merely a mate-of-all-trades, but a master of every one, with licenses to pilot ships up to fifty tons and tear down their engines, dive SCUBA to harvest sea cucumbers, and weld underwater. You name it, Rocky has passed the test—which didn't matter one whit to Kathy. The pair operated under the impression they were siblings, entitled to fond and wicked teasing.

With ship underway and introductions complete, we fishers slept. I woke briefly when Captain Dan dropped anchor just after midnight, listening as each great link of chain fell with a separate sound.

I woke again in darkness and came on deck at dawn. For an hour I watched slivers of silver salmon leaping along the shore. A bald eagle winged through low clouds, then swept down to perch on a deadfall. The tide was changing, shifting the balance of waters where a tongue of river met this mouth of the sea. Above a gray plane of water, black cliffs turned to a deep green blurred at the ridgelines by the boughs of evergreens. All the sound and movements around me, even the sharp slap of distant salmon, felt unusually smooth, quiet, enormous. I pondered this until the moment I smelled bacon.

Clearly the huge meal was meant to last us all day: eggs and pancakes, hot rolls and hash browns, enough breakfast meat that we hardly fought over the last three sausages. Then, as we all began to sink, Captain Dan said "Ready?" to Rocky, who said "Ready" back.

From the rear deck we watched the *Steller*'s boom turn to take up slack from a line tied to a buoy off the port side, then the winch began a grind that went on for many minutes. Even so, I was not prepared for the size of the wire cage that emerged from the depths to hang dripping above us, clattering with a crowd of captives. A solitary snow crab had a spread of twenty inches, but it looked minute among the score of kings, some of which had leg spans that looked wider than a yard.

"We eat well," said Captain Dan, even as Brian ordered us about, intent on arranging crabs in a flying-V formation for a photo shoot. After several takes, we dropped them into the aerated barrels where they would wait our pleasure.

Which was, then, to sail south, past the Icy Straits again, to Point Gustavus, then east through Icy Pass and into a gentle rain.

The Pacific side of West Chichagof and Yakobi Islands offers some of most scenic coastline in the world, a mosaic of steep-sided islands and islets and the water between these; narrow passages, broad, protected bays; secluded estuaries and fjords. The river systems draining these mountains rush down deep canyons; it may be ten miles from head-water to sea, or less than half that. Those streams with lakes in their courses likely nurture sockeye salmon, along with silvers, dog and humpbacks. It is said, without the surety of extensive surveys, that these waters constitute the last bit of steelhead range still untouched.

Without surety: that was the point, and part of the rationale for employing the *Steller* for this trip. Travel along this coast is difficult and can be dicey, requiring forays into open sea. Big commercial fishing boats troll for salmon along carefully restricted stretches of the ocean edge, but conditions there are too brutal for sportsmen's craft. Float-planes out of Juneau can hop between sheltered bays; but in the thousands of miles of shoreline between Gustavus and Sitka, there are few places to fuel or buy supplies.

Not a problem; the *Steller* seldom needs to shop. When we boarded, her tanks held enough diesel to reach Hawaii and return, some 6000 gallons. "I got fuel last month," Captain Dan said, "I won't fill again for four months." Long and wide as she is, however, the *Steller* draws less than ten feet, and is agile enough to twist through passes I could almost cast across. And slip in we would, carefully, to anchor in broader bays beyond these narrows.

That's when the *Steller*'s boom came into play. If I'd been impressed by how easily it lifted our loaded inflatables from the dock, I was delighted by the fact that we could launch them so swiftly—ninety seconds by the clock from at rest on deck to all anglers aboard and the outboard snarling.

Perhaps it took longer that first day, when we began the sequence we would follow with variations for the next four. We cruised down Lisanski Inlet to Lisanski Strait, past Islas Bay, through Imperial Pass into Portlock Harbor, to Goulding Harbor, then into the Goulding system south toward Pinta Bay. There we turned south again, toward Balc Bay, and an area so remote that "Cici is as close as you can get for a name."

All along this route we would search Dan's charts for rivers we wanted to look at, then sail close up through some majestic fjord, often through mists, sometimes seeing curls of steam rising off hot springs. From the top deck we would scope the river mouth to get a sense of the water, and to look for bears. If the former looked good and none of the latter appeared, or those present retreated convincingly, we'd launch the inflatables.

Usually we beached these at the river inlet. From there, personal patterns of action quickly developed. Rich and Brian tended to work the lower reaches, sometimes even casting to the estuary itself, while Aric and I followed upstream urges.

Part of the trick was to pick out silvers from schools of humpbacks and the occasional late-running dog salmon. Such discrimination was challenging when a pool seventy by thirty feet held 200 or 300 staging humpbacks, and perhaps only eight or ten of the quicker silvers; more difficult still, because of the dark skies and drizzle which came and went but mostly stayed.

From the first, Rich proved particularly adept at spotting the longer, torpedo-shaped forms with the black edges on their tails. He would stand stock-still in that predatory pose, watching for many minutes at a time, taut as a bow. Or he'd stalk rapidly down the bank, false-casting to keep line and fly airborne. "Silver," he'd hiss suddenly, then haul hard on the line as it pulled up tight to his loading rod. At the next forward sweep the fly would touch down, tucking into current just ahead of a shadow. Or shadows—those humpies. Another of Rich's talents was presenting his fly to only the intended, a silver, keeping it away from the "greedy" pack. If "one of those damn things" did take, he felt he'd failed.

From the first I had another perspective. California's trout get big enough, I am sure, but it's not every trip I tag a six-pound fish that is furious and determined and willing to fight ten rounds without sitting for the bell. True, humpbacks are the bantamweights of the salmon tribes; but like lighter fighters, they are speedy and stylish. True, also, that they are often easy to tempt. But so was I, in my youth; besides, they were not all easy, all the time. And though at first I caught them incidentally to silvers, for me they were a gratifying second place, still a prize. Especially the males.

That was another thing: I started learning something about the fish. I found that in the lower pools, where fish often crowded together in schools, it was the smaller, humpless females that would lunge for the fly, sometimes racing out six or eight feet to attack. But up in the riffles, as courting began, only males would strike—even abandon a mate to do so. I wouldn't let them take in such circumstances; once I lifted my fly off the water, the bucks would instantly return to their brides, presumably triumphant.

Of course, such studies were secret affairs, though I think Dan may have once seen me experiment. The Captain often accompanied us on our forays. Though not a recreational fisher—he thinks in tons—he's a committed naturalist who likes to look over new country, its flora and fauna. If I was close by, he would introduce plants like the dread Devil's club, and once he called me over to see a tree stripped of bark by the Hoona Indians, whose elders Dan had recently shepherded on a cruise to perform religious ceremonies at remote sites.

For obvious reasons, Dan kept a particularly close watch for bears. I think he found our attitude toward the bruins somewhat cavalier. His certainly wasn't, and he stood an uneasy watch whenever they were around or might be. This proved of singular value when a specimen we thought had abandoned his fishing grounds returned for a snack.

Most of these adventures were of two or three hours' duration. By then we'd usually be soaked through anyway; and it was soon wonderfully clear that Kathy had no intention of letting us pass through a day without the option of seven meals. Major events, like filet mignon with freshly baked bread and potatoes, a vast salad and lemon cream puffs, were separated by incidental affairs of roasted garlic with cheese and Greek olives, or perhaps a steaming vat of French onion soup, maybe some trifling smoked-salmon platter set on fennel sprays, with cream cheese and capers. And I do seem to remember a walnut raisin-bread fruit plate, a zucchini frittata, ceviche one day—and of course, there were often those king crabs, served up in a quesadilla, and in a chowder. . . .

"Float and bloat," as Brian liked to groan.

While we ate, our gear would tumble-dry and warm in the laundry, ready to go out again to the river we'd just left, unless we were already motoring out a pass to a new destination. In that case we-the-well-fed might join Captain Dan in the pilothouse, for lessons in the habits of otters, or sit at the booth in our room to tie flies. Somebody might heat himself to the bone in a hot shower; others would nap, knowing that we'd fish late after dinner, sometimes almost to ten P.M., and after that drink, tell stories, and laugh.

So it goes.

It was on that fifth day that I found my place in the world as Humpy King. But that was late afternoon, during the third of five forays.

While gearing up for the fourth, I noticed Rocky pestering the corroded innards of an ancient casting reel.

"Kathy wants a halibut," he grumbled. I nodded, noting to myself that the three-foot rod to which the busted reel was attached looked like some kind of kid's toy, last used to lift metal fish from a tub with a magnet. On our return, however, we found our mate and cook squabbling happily over credit for landing a fifty-pound slab still slapping on the deck, one of the big flatfish that come up the inlets to feast on salmon carcasses. All I could glean from their radically conflicting accounts was that the struggle had involved an undersized net, now busted; a small gaff, now bent; and a mop handle presently abbreviated by half. It is a stone fact, however, that the halibut ended up simmering in ginger.

At the last destination of that day the humpies were swarming in the lower pools. I hiked up over a high ridge, through berry bushes and rather too much bear sign. I was probably half a mile in before I bushwhacked down to the stream. Here it was about thirty feet across, shallow, with a bottom that looked black beneath a surface stippled by raindrops. I unhooked my fly from the keeper, and stepped in.

It was not a black bottom: it was absolutely solid with fish, so packed that the hundreds trying to flee me rose up on the backs of others, half out of the water, creating a thrashing wave that surged ahead and angled out to the sides. At every step the mayhem began again—upstream or down, no matter which way. . . .

I hooked the fly back to the keeper. Slowly, I waded down toward the estuary, creating havoc as I went, never casting. At last, even for me, there was no point to taxing my subjects.

Thus began the second stage of our journey. By moving so far south we had, we agreed, traveled from an area in which the humpback run was tailing off, to another where it was still in river-filling swell, with literally no room left for silvers. To go back would mean missing our look at all the waters ahead, among which Rich hoped to find at least a few that might produce steelhead next spring. Instead, we would continue, but now do our fishing for cohos in the estuaries themselves. Or, as Rich put it, angle for "silvers in the salt."

That is another story. It's enough to say here that the idea was to troll the fjords in our inflatables, waiting for strikes that would reveal a school. And to add to that Aric and I were often distracted by schools of "black bass," a rockfish with a remarkable resemblance to a freshwater largemouth that's been charred gray on a grill—and which happens to suffer from "'roid rage." The more we caught, the more would crowd about us, until once I took four fish in a row by holding the fly above the water, *without wetting the hook*. One after another they leaped out, caught the fly in the air, then somersaulted down.

It was while searching out these demons, trolling close to a tiny islet, that Aric and I met the sea lions.

Stellar sea lions: the females are almost the size of the average male of the species I've met in San Francisco Bay. Stellar males reach a ton. Aric told me it takes a taxonomist to tell one of their skulls from that of a grizzly. But unlike the glutted bears we had met, which barely favored us with glances, the sea lions sometimes paid us attention.

Rather too much, I noticed, as we moved slowly past a kelp bed within casting range of a rocky shore: ten or eleven females seemed to be following us. I pointed that out to Aric at the helm, then took out the camera he'd lent me to snap a shot.

"Isn't that interesting," he said pleasantly.

"Very," I agreed, as they moved to within a hundred feet. Now several of them were porpoising, making a peculiar kind of bark, which got louder as they came closer.

"Too interesting," I added encouragingly, while shooting again.

"Rather," Aric answered, and pushed our speed. "Let's just turn this little corner here . . ."

We did; they disappeared. After half a minute, we relaxed a little. "Big, aren't they?" I said—one of those rhetorical remarks.

As Aric grinned I noticed a small movement on an exposed rock nearby. A tiny flipper—a pup. "Well that's why. This is a rookery and they were only—"

Coming up. All of them at once, each one heavier than the boat and almost its length, thirty feet away, leaping and barking, falling with great crashes. In the photograph they don't fit the frame, and it was not a long lens— enormous gray shapes, blurred at the edges because just then Aric was gunning the outboard for all it was worth, heading toward open water with both of us clinging to a boat that's only a rubber bladder, really, our rods tucked behind us, like tails.

Two days later we were back at Gustavus Country Inn, arriving in time for dinner. A day after that, Rich and I barbecued salmon at his house in Juneau, then watched with smug expressions while our respectives made wet and greedy sounds inhaling the scraps of king crab we'd saved them. At some point, Lisa regaled me with the adventures she'd had with Sophie after I left—how the skies had socked in, so they'd stayed at the Whalesong, where the charming rooms all had Alaskan animal motifs. But the best part had been the whale watching.

Describing that, Lisa, who usually speaks a psychologist's version of a Southern California dialect, was positively effervescent, bubbling along at 78 rpm. For ease of reading I'll add punctuation:

"So they stop the engines and we drift, and the whales came right up to us! Right next to the boat! We were six feet, six feet I swear honest from this big one's eye! Eye to eye and he saw us I know he did—huge! And Sophie was right there looking at him, right there in my arms, completely unafraid! She did that little wave thing! And none of the people could believe she wasn't afraid and—"

"Did you tell them she was from Oakland?"

"I—what? No, of course not. What does that matter?"

I sighed wearily. "Dear, our daughter's from a tough place. Obviously she could tell that, unlike some of our neighbors, those whales were unarmed."

"Well . . . well, what an *annoying* thing to say."

I meant to suggest that she rephrase that remark, along the lines of "What an annoying thing to say, Your Majesty," by way of segueing into a discussion of my new status. But it struck me just then that being the Humpy

King has broader implications. Naturally Sophie will love being "Princess Pink." But Lisa, who was already revving up again on her manic travel narrative—

". . . so then we took the helicopter ride to the glacier, and Sophie is the very youngest person ever to ride in one—so beautiful!—are you listening to me? Why are you smiling? And why do you always come back from fishing so distracted?"

—Lisa, yes, was going to need some time, adjusting to the title of "Queen Hump."

4

Humpy King Meets Halibut God
One Year Later, on a Fjord South of Gustavus

I watched an eagle rake darker water near the river mouth, claw out a humpback salmon, rise with labored strokes. The buck whipped his body back and forth, snapping wildly; spawning hormones had caused his gums to shrink away from long canine teeth, creating fangs in a hooked kipe. He looked dangerous but was lost, held fast by talons impaling him through the swollen dorsal muscles that give his tribe their name.

The capture did not pass without comment. A gallery of seagulls screamed from the gravel delta below. Already glutted, they were tortured by the sight of another animal with food, and with three-note cries expressed their only idea: "Mine! Mine! That was mine!"

The eagle keened a reply that struck sharp echoes off the fjord's steep walls. Five-foot-wide wings caught a draft and angled up a slope too precipitous for the spruces and firs it supported, virgin giants growing right down to the water. I wondered what the inlet's name might be, but hadn't the faintest, just a sense that the seventy-foot *Steller* was now anchored somewhere south of the Icy Straits, not too far from the Myriad Isles, near to nobody.

"Good *work*." Rich's rubber boots slapped to a halt on the deck behind me. I turned to see him staring after the eagle. "That's one less humpy to bother me today."

I smiled at the implication, shook my head. "Seems a shame to me."

"You kidding? You can hardly get a fly to the silvers, for all the humps in the way. Like casting into commuter traffic."

"I know. But that fellow swam a thousand miles just to get lucky *once*, and now won't."

Rich gnawed on that. "Maybe you'd like a moment of silence?"

I laughed.

Humpbacks are the subject of our running debate. Rich Culver guides fly-fishing expeditions out of the elegant Glacier Bay Country Inn, in Gustavus. Like most hardcore anglers of this country, he disdains the humpback salmon, or "pink," preferring to pursue the larger, sleeker cohos, "silvers," and the enormous king salmon, also called chinooks. I live on a hill above a Walgreens in Oakland, and write about angling; on my first trip with Rich on the *Steller*, during an expedition to explore remote coastal streams, I'd asserted sovereignty as "The Humpy King," since only I seemed to appreciate their heart and single-mindedness. How could I not? These are four- to eight-pound fish that will flex a light fly rod clear through the cork rings. Often I'd battle a buck in some staging pool just above an estuary, release him, then watch as he surged upstream, wholly undeterred, determined as ever to nose the tail of some slim hen and ejaculate a cloud of milt onto her redd full of eggs. "Add a Led Zeppelin track and that could be me in high school," I'd told Rich.

To each his own.

Other anglers spilled out of the *Steller*'s galley, where cook Kathy had been warming their insides with sausages, eggs, flapjacks and good humor. Rich waved them toward the waiting Zodiac. First mate Rocky revved the outboard, then set off to ferry the party to the river, upstream as high as the tide allowed. Silvers came in with the flood; although we were too early for a solid run, in a week we'd caught and released scores.

"Sure you won't come?" Rich asked.

I nodded toward a boat rod I'd rigged with gigantic 9/0 circle hooks and five pounds of pink scraps. The day before, while we sports were playing upstream, Rocky and Kathy had landed limits of halibut, "chickens" of around fifty pounds.

"Lisa loves a halibut," I told Rich. "If I come home without any, I'll have less fun than that humpy when he gets to the eagle's nest."

Rich stamped back toward the galley for gear to load into the second Zodiac. I slipped a lever on the reel to let a pound of lead sinker drag my bait toward the bottom eighty feet down. I felt it bounce, thumbed back the lever, then jigged for a few minutes while watching a pair of ghostly jellyfish drift along the hull, pulsing, their mushroom heads canted into current. When the gulls started screaming again I looked up, half-expecting to see one of the fat brown bears we watched daily, *Ursus* so stuffed with salmon that they had the profiles of hamsters. No eagle, no bear, so for several minutes I scanned all the water I could see, from river mouth to the dark islands at the fjord's narrow opening to the sea, looking for sea lions or otters.

By then the morning's mist had cooled my coffee. That wouldn't do; I looped the braided Dacron line around a cleat to secure the rod while I trotted to the galley for a warmup. Rich swung out the door before I got there and, peering past my shoulder, said quickly, "You got a bite."

"Uh-huh. Kathy still have coffee?"

"I'm not kidding."

Neither was I, but sure enough, the top ten inches of rod bent down—less like a strike than a nod. I walked back and began to unwrap the Dacron from the cleat.

"Watch your fingers," called Rich.

Too late: for an instant one forefinger was pinned between taut line and cold metal. It hurt, then the line slipped off. "S'okay," I called back to Rich, then waited several seconds, feeding line. Ten feet later I hauled back to set the hook. The resistance felt solid, so I reared again, then a third time, still waiting for evidence that something live felt the steel.

It came, yanking me most of the way over the *Steller*'s rail, because the reel's drag was set too damn tight.

I shouted a series of Anglo-Saxon words, pushed backward, splayed my feet on the deck to brace myself, then used the railing as a fulcrum to lever the rod butt down. That worked for a moment, but I needed to let loose of the rod with one hand in order to turn the star-shaped drag adjustment on the reel. At exactly the instant I tried the fish pulled again. It also used the rail as fulcrum, of course, slamming the rod butt up into my testicles with a little less force than would shatter stones.

"The drag!" shouted Rich. "Let off the drag!"

"Gah," I replied. Then, in case I'd not made myself clear, "Gah . . . ohh . . . Gahhhhd."

"You got him? You okay? You got him!"

I chose not to answer this time, but with the rod tucked under my right armpit did manage the drag trick, which lessened the strain on the rig by allowing the fish to take line. I moaned in a manly sort of way, wondering, since when do halibut run like this? And how does a flat fish move so fast?

Rich had raced up to the rail and was now staring over the side as if to pierce the blue. He tested the tension of the line with a thumb, considered the rod's bend, then looked back into the depths. "This is the big one," he said. "This is it."

It seemed possible, but as I caught my breath I began to doubt. I'd never landed a halibut half the size of those I'd seen Rocky fillet the night before, so had no point of reference. And it's an embarrassment to overestimate the size of a fish, or to let someone else do so.

"No," I said. "Probably just like the others. I'm just not used to the tackle."

Rich shook his head. "No way."

"Rich!" called a booming voice, "You going ashore or not?

Captain Dan Foley, owner of the *Stellar*, gazed down from the bridge. Dan's almost six and a half feet tall, with a laugh and an intensity of attitude about the same size, an interesting admix of Maine man and John Muir.

"He's got the big one," Rich called back. "*The* big one. I mean it."

Dan studied the bend in my rod. "Yeah. Maybe so. Let me know when." He disappeared into the pilot house.

"Take your time," said Rich.

As if it was up to me: I couldn't even influence the direction of battle, I soon found, as the fish dragged me toward the bow with a series of four-foot-long surges.

"Is that its tail I'm feeling?" I demanded. "Those . . . *whumps?*"

" 'Fraid so," said Rich. "Like I said."

"No. Has to be regular-sized, Rich. I'm just getting old. Fat. I should stop smoking—"

"That won't help now."

"What I'm saying—"

For the second time a heave pulled me part way over the rail, not quite so far this time, but I grunted with the effort.

"*Mother*. This animal is—"

"Get the tip up!"

"Aft! Back—the stern! Clear those rods—"

"Easy! Take it easy!"

"*What is this thing . . . ?*"

"Hold *on*, man!"

I said nothing, but held. Line ran slowly off the reel spool. Stopped. Began to run again. Then to speed up.

Rich hissed. "Man . . . this fish is bigger than you are."

Time for another sea change of attitude. "Rich," I said softly, "This is bigger than both of us."

Halibut are not designed for long hauls at high speed, for battles of hours and the kind of bloody billfish ordeals that burst organs. Halibut ride tides for a living, hunting low, occasionally hurling their bulk upwards to attack. On the other hand, flatfish are all meat, which is muscle; and big ones boated before they are exhausted will break an angler's legs. So.

For fifteen minutes my fish hauled me about three sides of the boat, straining me into silence as lactic acid built to burning in my forearms and I began to wonder just who the hell was hooked here. Finally he came most of the way up—not close enough to see—then plunged all the way down again. I brought him up a second time, groaned silently as he dove, repeated the process once more. Rocky returned with the Zodiac sometime in there, and stalked about, grinning. As I winched the fish up a fourth time, he looked up to where Captain Dan stood watching. "Gaff," he said.

"You think so?" said Dan.

"Yep."

"No question," insisted Rich. "Make that a big gaff. Really."

"Make it three of 'em," said Rocky.

The water was deep emerald green with visibility of fifteen or twenty feet. I saw the shape rising, sucked air into my lungs, hauled. Up it came, still without reference, looking three feet long while only dimly defined. By the time I could make out an unblinking eye, I knew it was four feet, at least. Now the mottled brown skin began to develop definition and I could see the sickle-shaped maw. Still the fish grew.

Suddenly I had the strange sense that I was lifting into light a piece of the ocean floor. Which I was, in a way.

By the time the halibut looked seven feet long and was not yet at the boat we had all fallen silent. I have no idea what the others were thinking, but my mind had fixed on a single idea: *You don't catch things like this with a rod. You hunt them with packs of dogs.*

The fish tried to sound again, but now could not drive down its head.

Dan pulled out the gate on the rail, lay down on the deck, his right hand holding a two-foot steel hook. He looked waiflike compared to the fish.

"What do you want to do?" he asked me. "You want it, we'll try."

I couldn't take my eyes off the monster. "What's it weigh?"

"Two-fifty, two seventy-five. Who the hell knows? I haven't seen one like this in a while."

"It's eight feet long."

"I don't think so. Maybe. Your call."

When I shook my head, the image of Rocky shifted back and forth, but the memory of what he'd said the night before came into focus: "We try not to kill any over eighty-five pounds," he'd told me. "The giants are the best breeders, prime stock, fish you want to keep in the gene pool. It's just greedy to take them, that's all."

I'd read something about that once, some kind of geometric progression—that a twenty-kilo female produced x-thousand eggs, while one twice that size produced eggs by the millions. *Millions*.

That matters to me. Though I've caught fish ever since I can remember—worked fishing camps as a boy, have fished to feed my family, and am now a writer and editor for fishing magazines—I'm more admirer than predator these days. But there was something else involved here.

People take trophies for good reasons and bad. Mostly they want to preserve a triumph they're afraid they will otherwise lose. What I was feeling, however, was something ancient and visceral, an awe that was first cousin to both fear and reverence—an emotion that lives at the base of the brain. If it made no words it still proscribed, and I knew I would no more kill this fish for a picture, or to fill a freezer, than fell a 300-year-old Sequoia for kindling, or swat a hummingbird just to see it hold still.

"Cut it loose," I said to Dan.

He looked at me expressionlessly. Rich arched an eyebrow. Both said "You sure?" in very different ways.

"Yes. I'm sure. Cut it loose."

One quick cut.

For a moment, nothing changed. The halibut contin-ued to lie at the surface, mouth opening and shutting. Its dark eyes moved in their sockets, appearing to examine this alien world, relaying what it saw to a brain the size of a lima bean—but big enough. Another second, two; then the fish seemed to ripple. Once, twice. The tail turned up, hard; and the fish, still seeming to watch us, began to de-scend.

Rich looked at me. "Whoa," he said.

"Whoa," I replied. Then, after half a minute, I started to laugh. "I don't even know what that *was*," I said. Then, "I don't even know what that was *about*."

I still don't. But I have for all my time the image of that beast rising from its deep, and descending. I have sometimes imagined it moving in the dark, snapping the legs off king crabs and scavenging salmon carcasses as they drift toward the Pacific. I imagine it riding tides in the dark.

Lisa and I spawned Max less than ten months after I re-turned. He's off the charts in size. I like to imagine that had to do with the high-protein halibut meals we ate on my return.

Lord knows there was enough. Rocky brought me an ice chest full of fillets as I left the boat; Rich gave me more at the Glacier Bay Country Inn, after making me admit that he was right about the big one.

I had no problems with that. "Always humble," I said, "is the Humpy King."

5

Where We Learn These Things

Sophie and I strolled around the casting ponds. A woman was taking a lesson, probably her first. She was struggling, but it was her instructor who worried the Soph: at two years and seven months my daughter recognizes rude behavior, though I think she considers it the prerogative of people her size.

"Why, Daddy, why?" she whispered every time the teacher bellowed directions. Then she watched as he took the rod from his student and began to double-haul while announcing to everybody in the park and all the ships at sea, "You don't know lucky you are to have *me* be the one that's showing you this stuff, the *right* way."

Really.

"Why, Daddy?"

"Because the man is a twit."

"What's 'twit'?" Once is all I have to say a word, if it's nasty.

"In this case it's like that spot under Misha's tail that you're not supposed to touch, but bigger and bright red— look at the squirrel! Look—look—oops, he's gone. Let's go find a pine cone."

We did, but only one of us was distracted. I sat on a bench, watching Sophie investigate twigs while chastising myself for providing her an image she might sometime pass on to polite company. Eventually that musing prompted a memory of my own parents, and a lesson I learned a long time ago.

Never mind what it says in some rotting manila folder, I did not call my second-grade teacher a son-of-a-bitch. At that age I was obliged to idolize Mrs. Madison, so was only dismayed when she believed the outrageous report of some snitch—especially since it was the snitch himself whom I'd described with my father's most violent oath. But Mrs. Madison swallowed that twit's tale whole, and raged, as was her inclination anyway. Not only was I suspended from school, but she also insisted that my parents meet with her to discuss my crime.

The prospect filled me with dread. Despite the words my father occasionally used for emphasis, both my parents had elegant manners, and in our family respect was important enough to encourage with an open palm to the hind end. Worse yet, both my mother and father were teachers themselves, of the most devoted kind.

I still remember the long walk to our old Mercury after that meeting. A frenetic mirage of heat waves rose off the asphalt and my parents looked at least as hot. Silently, my father opened the car door, folded the seat forward, waited for me to climb in. He shut the door, then stood and listened as my mother spoke to him with great urgency. I believed she was trying to convince him not to spank me *completely* dead, and prayed for her success.

They both got in the car, then stared at me over the seat back. "You know better," said my father evenly.

"I do?" I said, confused, still unwilling to confess a crime I'd not committed.

"Yes, you do. Mrs. Madison is a woman. She cannot be a 'son.' "

What?

"Micky," said my mother sternly. Then, to me, "You don't know this yet, dear, but some people . . . should not teach. Because not *everyone* should be a teacher. Do you understand?"

I didn't.

"Particularly a royal bitch like Mrs. Madison," said my father.

"*Micky*," my mother snapped. And to me: "That's a word for lady dog, but don't use it. Do you understand?"

No, again. But I did grasp something more important—*I wasn't going to get spanked*.

"Yes ma'am," I said, with the pent-up intensity of relief.

When I went back to school two days later, it was to a new class.

Some people should not teach.

The casting instructor was now working out more line. He could throw, no question about it. Maybe he understood the physics as well, the relation of rod and line to moving body parts. Perhaps he had the tools to communicate technique. Even so, there's another trait a teacher needs, so vital that without it students will be lucky to learn by accident. It's difficult to describe simply, but try calling it Vicarious Ego, the ability to take profound satisfaction from somebody else's success. In a situation like this lesson, a good instructor would walk away happy— truly gratified—if convinced that through the exercise of his wisdom and skill this student left these ponds a better caster, prepared for the challenge of a stream. It would not be sufficient, for a *good* instructor, merely to believe that he had impressed this woman, and dazzled the world with his braying.

Luckily, there are just such fine teachers in the fly-fishing world, people with adequate knowledge and benign motivation. Some of them charge for their services, which is fine and fair; others mentor for free. At the same ponds where Soph and I wandered, for instance, members of the Oakland Casting Club have trained generations of anglers, standing stalwart beside bodies who may begin a Saturday morning thrashing and end with a stroke which presents a fly well enough to raise a fish—voluntarily, I mean, instead of through percussive trauma. One kind fellow from this outfit even offered to tutor me through the year he estimated it would take to remedy errors I've ingrained over decades. He swallowed hard at the prospect, however; I declined in the end. He was an older gent, after all, and although he seemed in excellent health, I feared the effect; at the very least, my groans would have damaged his hearing.

Tying is another area where expertise comes at an investment of time. With assistance, the fundamentals of palmering hackle can be learned quickly; without, the process can leave you hating chickens. I first tried it at ten or eleven years of age and was so discouraged I waited most of my lifetime for a second go—too bad, given that tying, even as crudely as I do, turns out to be one of the more settling activities I've found, a superb way to focus the sort of kinetic energies which suggested to Mrs. Madison (and her successors, to be fair) that Ritalin was in order.

Then there are bugs. The study of our prey's prey—which obviously includes also crustaceans and baitfish, worms and assorted eggs, even mammals—is an area in which teachers are rarer, partly because those who know what's important about this subject do not, rightly, consider themselves entomologists or aquatic biologists. (And perhaps a few who might otherwise serve well have grown overfond of Latin.) If you can find somebody able and willing to sort out beasts for you, trail them around as long as they'll let you. Offer to carry vials and collecting equipment; liquor them up, if you must, but save some of the clear spirits for preserving specimens.

Which leaves reading water—so difficult, so critical; properly preparing gear, because most of the time leader construction is more important than the micro-tolerances of your reel; and an assortment of other skills all the way out to the near ethereal realm of splitting cane for rods, if that's where you want to go.

So much to learn. Such an advantage to have a sage who can show you.

Neither of my parents could teach me fly fishing, as it happens, nor could anybody else that I knew, so that early tying debacle wasn't my only frustration. For twenty years I proceeded on my own, picking up bits and pieces, reinventing many wheels not nearly round. I gleaned a little from sporting magazines, though for my life I couldn't learn knots from a page.

Mind you, there's nothing terribly wrong with this solo approach. I certainly enjoyed myself. On the other hand, most years you could comfortably roll a log up the three-degree incline of my learning curve; and I do wonder what it might have been like if I'd had access to somebody who could roll-cast, and had any interest in teaching me to.

I did get a glimpse of the possibilities a while back, when a friend who manufactures tackle gave a speech at a fly-fishing club. Speaking before a group obviously made him uncomfortable; yet it was apparent that there was something he very much wanted to say.

It had nothing to with the products he makes and sells. Instead, he took this public opportunity to thank a man who had taken him fly fishing many, many times when he was growing up, on a Sierra stream which still runs bright with memories. Soon we were all moving with the current of his gratitude, and, like him, mourning the passing of a generous soul.

My friend's speech also provided me with an insight: he's one of those fly fishers who are always ready to help anybody who asks. *Aha*.

It wasn't quite an accident that he's a member of the same club I heard the blowhard casting master begin to denigrate, in a manner more devious and profane than any oath.

I smiled to hear him. I have also taught, for twenty years now, beginning in a remote Southeast Asian fishing village, continuing to this day on a locked psychiatric ward. I have both an appreciation for anybody who wants to learn, and respect for the intelligence of students. Ignorance of a subject, like how to cast a fly line, does not imply a leaden mind. This lesson in front of me was almost over. The student knew more about her teacher than what he was supposed to teach; and I had a plan of action.

When I caught up with the woman at her car, I was wearing Soph on my shoulders. "Lady fisher!" my daughter cried.

The woman's tight smile suggested she might not feel deserving of the title. I thought, "If ever a student of mine leaves class looking like this. . . ."

What I said was, "She will be pretty soon, I bet. Now, Sophia, please give the lady fisher the card you have for her."

"No," said Soph. "It's mine."

"I'll give you another."

"No."

"I will give you *two*."

"Okay," said Sophie. "Here, lady!"

The woman took it.

"On the front," I said, "there's the address of a magazine I work for, which you might find of interest. On the back are a couple of phone numbers, in case you ever want to join a club."

I saw her recognize a name she'd heard spoken just five minutes before. "I think I've . . . heard of this one," she said cautiously.

I laughed. "Is that a fact. Well, the truth is that there are any number of ways to learn fly fishing. Clubs have speakers, classes and outings, libraries, people who can be awfully helpful. They usually have good relationships with shops. As to whether you'd like this club, or another one, or any at all . . . that's a very *personal* sort of decision. *Very* personal, you understand."

She nodded slowly.

I felt Sophie twist on my shoulders. "Daddy," she whispered.

I turned. The casting instructor was watching us from his truck parked across and down the street.

"The *twit!*" said Sophie excitedly.

"What?" said the woman.

Once, I swear to God, is all it takes.

"He *is*," Sophie said to her. Then she leaned forward to continue, with devastating sincerity, "You know, *like the one my cat Misha has under his tail!*"

I felt all sorts of color rising into my cheeks. The woman looked stuck between horror and laughter.

"Kids," I said weakly. "You've got to wonder where they get these things."

Laughter won the lady. Sophie and I went off to find chocolate, and swings.

6

Hazards of the Fly

Slave, I have set my life upon a cast
And I will stand the hazard of the die.

—William Shakespeare
King Richard III, Act V, Scene IV

The Audubon Bird Clock announced two A.M. with the call of a black-capped chickadee, and I could still feel the hum of Interstate 5 in my belly. As usual the drive home through the Central Valley had coated my skin with a slick of diesel fuel and dust, adding those to films of fly floatant, trout slime, line dressing, and the odd dribble of Whopper *du jour*. A scalding shower was the first thing I wanted on my return. I peeled in the bathroom, quietly, so as not to wake the sleeping Sophie, who at the age of two years and seven months is a Stalinist. I caught a bleary glimpse of the pink V of sunburn on my chest, then—

—*what is that?*

The scab was about the size of a split pea, high on the right side of my deltoid, pinkish gray and bulging. Around a ring of rust-colored blood the skin was swollen and flushed and warm to the touch. It looked a little like a puncture wound, which was not unlikely; for much of two days I'd bushwhacked up a tiny creek, taking my licks between plunge pools, using the streambed to skirt deadfalls and boulders. Sometimes I had to go up and over and I must have scored myself on a dozen branches, never mind the blackberry brambles. Several times I found myself unusually concerned about my eyes—not worried exactly, but conscious of what a long haul out it would be, hiking back to the road half blind.

The fish were worth it, rainbows of five inches and even seven, one massive specimen an inch shy of ten. Redbands, I'm pretty sure, with crisply defined crimson bars, spots hard-edged and black as the bits of obsidian called Apache Tears—sleek trout so wild it seemed like energy burst from their bodies. Maybe it does, and in the right spectrum of light they throw blue sparks. . . .

Perhaps, in my fascination with these fish and the adventure they offered, I'd not noticed receiving this stab. Now it was infected.

Shoot, I thought irritably, and scratched at the scab.

Irritably, the scab's legs twitched, and clawed for new purchase.

Aww, no.

Ah, yes. Once again, there was a price for angling indulgence, including this time the long wait for a bull's-eye rash that never showed. But that's how it goes, for such as we, Wild Things, Fly Fishers Who Boldly Face Hazards of the Fly.

Come again? you say.

Until Brad Pitt hurled himself into Class III white water to land a trout in *A River Runs Through It*, fly fishers had a popular image about as macho as that of tournament bowlers—and who cared? But suddenly, people who'd been merely amused by our eccentric "hobby" were sidling up to remark, "Gosh, those rivers are so pretty. But do you really jump into rapids, to chase after fish?"

"Not *every* time," I'd answer honestly.

"What?"

Okay, so I got a kick out of seeming daredevil. And long have I worried about angling's serious lack of groupies. Moreover, Pitt's plunge reminded me of a time, ten years ago now, when I first considered the perils of fly fishing, a contemplation that had also begun with a pose.

It was a Christmas when I was trapped in an Eastern Sierra condo with skiers from Los Angeles—though I had done nothing wrong. Whoa-dudes and radical risk-takers, my companions relentlessly taunted each other to perform stunts very likely to end in paraplegia. Appropriately enough, each time one survived an effort he celebrated with high-pitched cries, falsetto yips suggesting the drastic atrophy of his testicles.

I found this of purely academic interest, of course, since I spent my time angling the lower Owens River; also, I have a secret affection for people whose inability to consider death leads to early organ donation. Unhappily, my digression from *LA norm* annoyed them, as I learned during their evening meditation over brews.

"Hey, man," said one, with what passes for a sneer in people with excellent orthodontia. "Like, fly fishing's not even a *sport*."

"Of course not," I replied pleasantly. "It's much more intense."

"Where's the *rush*, man?" said another.

Of course, I tried to describe the aspects of fly fishing that engage me: arts, skills and science, allure of wild creatures and places—the usual. And someday I hope to preach the Golden Rule to *Hezbollah* bombers—I mean, here I was talking aesthetics to people whose sport requires clear-cutting mountains, and who dressed by brand names in the colors of bass plugs—chartreuse, hot pinks, many exciting perch patterns. Suffice it to say that soon I realized that in order to survive the *après trout* hours, I needed a change of tactics.

"Why fly fish?" I wondered rhetorically, the next time I was confronted, employing the sort of artificially outsized voice their people used when communicating, along with phrasing that goes heavy on glottal stops. "Like, that's what I ask myself, every time I go, you know. Wish I could tell you that it's pretty and all. But the dirty truth is . . . I just love the adrenaline rush."

"What?"

"Right. There's nothing like it. But, hey, you guys should have a grasp. I mean, maybe skiing's not so dangerous as fly fishing, but you must get *some* thrill, near the top of those expert runs, right?"

"*Danger? In fly fishing? What* danger, man?"

"I *know*," I replied ruefully. " 'What danger *this* time?' is what I ask myself every time I go out. Like, will I risk death from falling, or drowning—or both? Hypothermia and frostbite? Or dehydration and heat stroke? Will I run into rattlesnakes, like on the Verde and Big Salty? Or more alligators like on the Santee Cooper? Or maybe I'll think about that sea snake in the Bora Bora lagoon. And sometimes I remember that python I saw fishing the paddy country in Malaysia; I still dream about that. Jeez . . ." I shook my head, obviously bewildered at my own folly. "Those scorpions along the Colorado River near Yuma— you'd think I'd learn, you know? How about that night of dancing tarantulas on Canyon Lake? Or the time I caught Portuguese man o' war tentacles across my eye and arms in the Sea of Cortez—when the numbness spread to my chest, so it got hard to breathe? Forget those fat Alaskan brown bears, or that cougar near Loon Lake, it was the wolverine above Tule Lake that still flips me out."

Another rakish grin, then a shoulder shrug to acknowledge how utterly helpless I was, lost to this self-destructive obsession. "I mean, I got to tell you that so many times, I'm really grateful fly fishers get to wear rubber pants." Another shrug and a head shake, then I let my eyelids fall half way, doing adolescent angst. "But that's how it goes, man. Like, I am what I am; can't nobody change me."

About that time my baffled skier provocateurs were ready for another Coors, or maybe one of their group Jacuzzi baths, in which they would simmer for hours, looking a little like tripe. I have no idea what they were thinking, of course. But I hoped they regretted their safe little lives.

I contemplated mine the next morning, while laying out a roll cast on the Owens and savoring the previous evening's incident. Eventually I began rehashing the incidents I'd reported. Slowly and a little uneasily, I began to puzzle. There was a rub, you know.

Like most fishers who've been at it a while, I've taken bad falls, come too close to worse ones. I've gone under while wading in current, suffered both frostbite and hypothermia, been dehydrated and watched my vision fade with heat. I killed an insanely aggressive rattler on the Verde and did encounter wary alligators on the Santee Cooper. In Bora Bora's lagoon I watched a stingray the size of a Cadillac hood swim straight at me from forty feet away, slipping through fourteen inches of water to release at my feet a live sea snake it was dragging in its mouth. (Judging by the snake's terrified reaction to me, it was having a bad-scale day.) You probably shouldn't believe that happened, but yes, I came across five *yards* of python—or it came across me—in a river just below Thailand, where other reticulated serpents can run to twenty-five feet. Years ago I brushed a scorpion off another Boy Scout's heinie; and while camped on a desert reservoir one night I sat on a boulder—way up on a boulder—to watch a waltz of mating tarantulas. It was in 1979 that I saw the mountain lion, only for a moment, out at Loon; '91 when the Portuguese man o' war stunned me; and only last year when I fished for an hour within a couple of double-hauls of a salmon-gorged grizzly. (As to the wolverine—never mind, even I don't buy that story, and I was there.)

In other words, I had not lied, not even exaggerated much, save by suggesting I enjoyed cheating death.

I don't, although I certainly prefer it to the alternative. Fear just isn't an exciting part of any game I enjoy; I won't even go to horror movies, so whatever anxiety or injury I suffer while fishing are prices I pay reluctantly, as seldom as possible. Maybe I will edge along a ledge if there's no other way to get at a good fish, or wade above my waist in water wherein a misstep means a dunking; but probably not. Feeling fear just isn't the point. You want daring? Walk from my house to the Walgreen's on High Street near Macarthur at 11 P.M. to pick up Sophie's earache medication. Want to double the risk? Wear a Rolex Oyster and a pair of Bali shoes. Nevermind "extreme skiing," make the gamble mean something: test the AIDS vaccine, teach high school. I mean, on the New Year's Day after my Christmas-cum-ski-bum I worked a double shift on a locked ward, running four violent restraint procedures. So on vacation, I should risk my life *for sport?*

Nah. And yet we fishers do. Incidentally, usually; and driving is still, I'm sure, the most hazardous part of any trip. But the sense that all our adventures are sans jeopardy because we court fish, not risk, doesn't wash; and you could certainly compose your own laundry list of dangers you've already survived, others you hope to, with a little luck and preparation.

Which is not a bad idea, really. At least to list such hazards in your head, then take a moment as the engine warms to consider whether you're ready for each. First-aid kit, water and spare food, a space blanket . . . tick them off, one by one.

Make one a gray tick, why don't you, like the one I found at two in the morning. Many anglers, and most who bushwhack, have had them or will; and where are your good tweezers right now? Or do you think you'll use your hemostats? None of the dime-store witcheries work for me, not hot matchheads nor kerosene nor rubber cement, but a slow pull with tweezers usually does it.

Not this time. This verminous creature had literally lost its head. I believe it forgot it was simply looking for a meal and decided to burrow. Whatever the reason, it was very, very deep.

First those little legs tore off, then the body, but still the whole head remained embedded below the skin. Nothing left to do but to call the advice line for my notorious HMO. I expected a "Get back to us when the arm has maggots," but the ER nurse's daughter has Lyme disease, so she insisted I come in the next day, when a nurse practitioner remarked that she'd "never seen a tick dig in quite like this." She scheduled surgery two days later, which seems soon, unless you have some bug's head rotting in your flesh.

The surgeon, a Scotsman, spent a lot of time carving, it seemed to me—and have you noticed that any substance with a name that ends in *-caine* stings a lot? He mentioned the rash, assured me that most Lyme-carrying ticks are the size of a pin-head, then advised, "Next time, do wear long sleeves."

I had been—two shirts.

"Well then, perhaps you will consider staying out of the woods where you find such things."

"Not likely," I said. When he looked disapproving, I asked what he did for sport.

"Rugby, used to. And of course, in the winter, the wife and I ski."

"In other words, Doctor, you play life safe," I came within millimeters of saying. But I didn't; like other fly fishers, I hesitate to insult people holding switchblades, straight razors, or scalpels.

7

⚜

Lion in the Grass

⚜

On my desk are nine photos a better cameraman would not have shot, as darkness drew down on a meadow stream. Two pictures are badly blurred, but in all the rest you see that the buffalo grass has been bleached to straw and gone to seed and that a fisher wearing only tan shorts and a slung leather bag is burned dark on his shoulders and back. In one image the tawny man exactly matches the color of his split-cane rod.

It's a Robert Sigman 2-weight, a seven footer, on one of the first evenings the fisher used it. At his insistence I'd cast it several times, but he stood close by, twitching a little and repeating "Can you feel it?" over and over. I thought I could, but he was clearly falling in love. "You do feel it, don't you?" he said as I handed it back. One of his eyebrows arched with inquiry, like the wing of a small bird, but his whole body relaxed when the rod passed safely back into his hands. "I know you do," he said. "Manifestly."

Maybe I cocked my head at that. *Manifestly:* I'd met him only hours before and already understood that he put words in places I would not expect to find them—important words, large with meaning. He seemed to savor their sounds as he said them, like a craftsman who's creating art by adding flourishes to the mundane, elements intricate and surprising.

"I feel it," I said. "It's a lovely piece of work."

He smiled. "Isn't it, though? And now, if you don't mind. . . ."

"Please," I said, then he was off to catch the last hour of light and a brown he'd staked out earlier that day.

I don't know why I followed him. Fish were moving and I'd caught a few, but for some reason I traded rod for camera to trail him upstream, staying well back from the bank so as not to spook his fish. Maybe I believed he really was going to catch a big fish and I wanted to watch. I did watch: he moved through the meadow with an excited tension he seemed barely to contain, slowly, stepping softly, utterly absorbed. I remember thinking *That's the way to do it*—stripped down in a summer evening, slipping through the grass, smelling water and listening for a rise. At some point I marked the contrast between us, with me waddling about in my neoprenes and overstuffed vest.

I don't remember why I followed him, but I bet I know what he would say. The gist of it would resemble the kind of things he'd said earlier, when we first met and he was hiking me around this ranch where he was building a cabin. He'd heard I was a writer, and constructed from my vocation and whatever he saw in my face a too-marvelous image, a vision really, of a man with a spiritual connection to water and woods, who loved ideas and had a fascination with language.

He wove other charitable suppositions into our discussion as we walked along the creek, sliding these between

observations of subtleties in current, hatches I could expect, the locations of undercut banks. It was pleasant but
briefly confusing; I did not think that this was about me;
nor was it flattery. At last I decided, and was convinced,
that he was revealing himself, projecting his own image
onto mine, seeing there the man he hoped I might be.
This curious vignette he created was of him, and however
misdirected, was also thoughtful, gentle, and kind. Parts
seemed dreamy, almost a rapture, especially when he contemplated the relationship between nature and man, or
between nature and what I might call the soul.

"You know what I'm saying," he would remark every
so often. "Of course you do. I know you've thought
through all this, I can sense it. And listen to me go on."
Then he would, wondering aloud and with pleasure about
the world as we found it. At last, he laughed. "You want to
go fishing, I can feel that too. It's like a hunger in you." He
nodded. "I know just how that feels."

I fished. Some hours later he hiked out to find me
again, show me the rod, have me cast it. Then he said "if
you don't mind" and I followed him with the camera.

It looks like I shot photographs in two batches. There's
more light in the first group of six, though not enough. It's
a series: he approaches the bank in a crouch, kneels in
grass almost waist high. He strikes a fish. The rod arcs left
in one shot, way right in another. In the one where he
makes a release, he's a blur. The fish never appears save as
a splash, but I remember it was a rainbow.

He didn't get his brown that night. He has since,
though, landing him with that honey-colored wand of rod.
I hear it was about nine pounds.

The second batch of photos was taken with a flash,
though in one of them the sky glows pink and purple
above the mountains behind him. The best one is missing,

I hope because I gave it to him. But the three I have are striking anyway, however poorly framed. Because of the grass, and the darkness, I suppose, they look a little like pictures from Africa, of savanna at night, and a lion.

I woke the next morning smelling grass and hearing a distant clinking sound. A hundred yards away from my camp, my host was lifting weights. He did a lot of that, I found out, along with hiking up mountains and swimming lakes every day.

That evening we had dinner, four of us, sitting in the half-built A-frame. I don't remember what we laughed about, but I did discover that he was positively a fiend with a router: practically every plane had a contour cut into it—the craftsman as artist. Manifestly.

We've met several times since, at a lodge he manages. When the schedule allows, he disappears into the mountains for days at a time, by bike or on foot, wearing about as much as when I saw him fish the meadow. If he takes the 2-weight I suppose it fishes waters not often touched: be sure they're touched gently. I imagine him connecting to them and everything else up there, describing scenes to himself with a smile and superlatives. During the winter, he and his lady often travel to remote places. When at the lodge, he swims the lake there, days when it's not frozen over.

About a year ago, on the bank of that lake, we had another talk, mostly about nasty practices in the fly-fishing business. A remark he made set me musing; last January I passed him the short story that came of that, a complete fiction in which one character has a trait or two that I thought would make him smile.

The last time I saw him he'd just finished reading it. He did smile, and arched one of those eyebrows at me.

"Some night," he said, "you and me are going to sit down and talk about this."

I laughed. "We will," I promised.

I remembered that promise a few days ago, when I got word that the story comes out soon. I thought to visit him, then dug around for these photographs. Studying them reminded me of a summer evening I've wanted to describe for a long time. It means something, an epiphany, distilling in a moving image a moment when there's nothing between a man and wildness and they meet at his skin, when he's prowling through a Nature by which he defines his own, and wherein he feels close to what I would call a soul.

And I tell you, that man looks to me for all the world like a lion in the grass.

There was another reason this piece was written at the time that it was: I was told that Kevin Anderson was dying.

A draft of this manuscript was sent to him. According to Louise Gardener, whom Kevin proudly called "My Lady," Kevin did read it. She says he hoped to talk to me about it. I hope we have that chance, but it won't be this time around.

He remains forever a Lion in the Grass.

8

*****

A Crime of Passion

*****

"**Y**ou can relax now. But when the time comes, our hearts will be pounding. I promise."

The speaker nods his head for emphasis. His resemblance to Valentine Atkinson is truly startling. Of course, the real Atkinson is one of our sport's premier photographers, the kind of guy who has fished everywhere you hope to, hit grand slams with giant permit and 120-pound tarpon, hammered peacock bass in some jungle. So if this was him—for the sake of easy reference, let's just pretend—and you heard him talking about a heart-pounding angling adventure that he would photograph if Someone Else served as subject and writer while Somebody kept watch for cops . . .

. . . you'd certainly listen carefully. Especially since this would happen in a place only a bus ride and a misdemeanor away.

Your misdemeanor, as it happens.

77

The fellow next to Val is attentive, that's for sure. Author, first-tier editor of an awesome magazine and would-be lookout, he also nods, revealing with that gesture an elegant economy of motion: he agrees *and* his lips fall to the rim of a martini glass recently refilled with cucumber vodka. It's just the kind of nod-and-drink thing some people would associate with Richard Anderson, King of *California Fly Fisher* magazine, whom we've met.

I imitate him, of course, as would any writer. The cold cuke juice isn't half bad. In fact, it's good enough to make me philosophic: Val's right, I decide, I am relaxed, partly because I've decided that when I report this story, I'll call myself Ambrose Bierce. That's a Writer's Prerogative.

Richard nods again. "What we really need is a shot of (Ambrose Bierce) in handcuffs, as the cops lead him away."

That's Editor's Prerogative, apparently—and exactly the third time Richard has made this suggestion, which is making me edgy. I even sneak a look around the tables near ours, mindful of other ears. Probably not a problem: the Infusion Bar and Restaurant, tonight's Command Central, caters to those barely post-pubescent business types who can afford four-dollar drinks and fifteen-dollar entrees. It's an unlikely place for The Law to lay in ambush for urban guerrilla anglers, who are a mainly Popov bunch, when it comes to vodka.

Meanwhile, Val is measuring between his hands. "I mean, these fish are like this. They look smart, and the water's pretty clear. I experimented with them today, with bread and broccoli."

I can't help myself. *"Broccoli?"*

"Right. It's what I had in the 'fridge. They would rise for it—"

"Really?"

"Yes. But they'd usually spit it out. I think they like bread better."

Richard may or may not be mumbling about handcuffs again, but I am charmed and intrigued. Vegetable chum. And grains—two basic food groups. This is particularly important information, since I'm supposed to tie flies for this trip. Whole wheat I can do with clipped deer hair. But, "What made you try *broccoli?*"

Val looks slightly put off. "Like I said, I had it in the 'fridge. And the day before they were eating algae. So . . ."

"It matched the hatch?"

"Yes. Right. More or less."

I can't emphasize enough how interesting I find this, but I don't want to be rude. Instead, I launch a vaguely pedantic monologue on carp.

Right, carp: technically the biggest of "minnows," family Cyprinidae, evolved in southeast Asia, emigrated throughout Europe, and were eventually imported to this country from England by a German entrepreneur in the late 1800s. Washington politicians immediately declared them "miracle fish," and offered live stockings to districts that voted their direction. Pay-offs were shipped across the country by train in containers previously holding pig parts—thus, I believe, the evolution of the phrase "pork-barrel politics."

Precisely because they *are* miracle fish, carp survived these grim journeys; when it comes to breathing, these fish can make do with a moist Handi-wipe. For one thing, their blood contains a unique form of hemoglobin, which traps oxygen with unparalleled efficiency. For another, when utterly deprived of usable oxygen, carp begin to self-ferment, producing alcohol—

"What proof?" demands the editor.

"What?"

"What proof? This alcohol they're making."

—which they break down into sugars, then energy. One Indian cypranid, *Resbora daniconius*, lasted 102 days while hermetically sealed in a tube, losing 75 percent of its body weight before succumbing.

That suggests carp are among the hardiest of fish. Consider them also among the easiest fed, omnivores that can eat almost anything we do, even *after* we have. Large eyes with many cells in the retina help them find their food; they also have excellent hearing, listening through their big swim bladders. According to one study reported in *The New Compleat Angler,* carps' memories are so good they learn mazes as well as laboratory rats. No wonder that *Smithsonian Magazine* insists they are now the most ubiquitous fish in North America.

North America, it so happens, is also the only continent where carp are widely despised. Worldwide, more tons of carp are farmed for food each year than any other freshwater fish. Japanese *koi* are carp, which means that some specimens are the most pricey fish anywhere, maybe the most expensive items with fins, excepting only the Concorde. Carp are so admired by English coarse anglers that these folks practice a kind catch-and-release ethic requiring that Violators Shall Be Hurt By Fanatics in Groups.

"Where did you get all this?"

It's possible the editor's eyes are glazed like that out of admiration.

It's possible.

"I did a piece for *Field & Stream*. In '89 or '90, I think."

Val nods politely. "Do you have a solid-color shirt? Blue would be good. About this blue." He points to some crockery. When I make a noncommittal noise, he and the editor agree that one or the other will provide my clothing. I am mildly offended, and sulking because I never got to the part about carp's life span—somewhere between fifty and 100 years—or their fecundity, which I recall as around 400,000 eggs per pound of female. Then I remember the broccoli, and am happily distracted.

". . . the key" I hear Val saying, "is to get an editor to commit to paying our bail and fine."

"Absolutely," says Richard. "I'll go as high as five dollars."

"There we go, then. I did check, by the way: there's no sign prohibiting fishing. None."

I like that. "Then it's not a problem. They have to warn you."

Richard demurs. "Ignorance is no excuse."

"All right, all right. Then we'll tell them we're doing an article, just experimenting, la-la-la."

"No way," says Richard firmly. "It's got to be something any of our readers can get away with. That's the *point*." An editor, heart and soul, I tell you. "We'll claim we were practice-casting," he continues, "and caught fish by accident."

Certain kinds of people miss details and the same sort often run late, so I do and I am on the morning we've set for the expedition. I'm also cranky, after noticing in the mirror that my beard is going gray in streaks. This evidence of aging provokes striking realizations. The first is that I started sneaking around to fish for carp during the Eisenhower administration and continued right through Nixon's second term. During that era, I must have been nabbed on forbidden waters twenty times. Inevitably, capture led to threats of arrest, fines, and worse. What saved me then was that even notoriously nasty security guards, like those at the Phoenix Zoo, seemed to feel foolish about the idea of marching such a small miscreant "Downtown," accompanied, as I would have been, by "Exhibit A: Fishing Handline Wrapped Around a Fat Pencil."

But that was then, my mirror suggests. I suspect those same fellows would react differently today, when even *I* consider me suspicious-looking, or at the very least, unnecessarily hirsute.

I am ruminating along those lines when it strikes me that never mind my Beirce *nom de plume*, with Valentine shooting pictures this same streaky gray mug could end up on a full-page shot. Me, and a carp—"The Carp and I"—snout to snout, swarthy together and bound forever in an image somebody somewhere will save for official purposes. As in, The Library of Congress.

I decide to BART over to SF. When a woman sees me riffling fly boxes, she elects to sit beside me, in order that we might chat about her ex-husband. A "fly-fishing maniac," she says grimly, glaring with eyes in which the pupils might be slightly oval, elongated on the vertical axis. "That's all he did and all he was good for. That's *it*. Is that the same for the rest of you?"

A wee challenge. Her expression is familiar because a pal of mine kept a ferret. I briefly consider telling her I haven't *been* "the rest of us" yet. Then I have a better idea, good practice for the cop I may meet later. "I'm not sure," I reply with a warm smile. "But perhaps late some night you'll want to find out . . . and I am in the phone book. Anderson is the name. That's Richard, with an R."

Val has laid out sweet rolls and coffee. By way of easing into the criminal mentality, we dribble crumbs while walking around his apartment, ogling exhibits of antique or treasured tackle, his hat collection.

And fish photos, of course. In his living room there's one shot of him grappling a billfish, another of that *Fly Rod & Reel* cover where he and a guide hold between them a tarpon the size of kayak. Standing directly in front of these, Val says "I've been watching those carp every day—they are a-*ma*-zing. Just monsters. This is going to be fantastic. Are we *really* ready?"

He's dead serious. We're getting there, too. First, the rod selection.

Val shoots for and represents a company, but that's not the reason both choices carry that brand name. "I have stacks of these," he explains. One is too perfect for our purposes, an older eight-foot 4-weight that breaks down into five pieces—five, count 'em—and actually fits in my canvas briefcase, strung up and ready to fly. The reel is a 300-dollar clunker. "Stuff must be expendable. So we can pitch it, if we have to, or in case they take it away from us."

For my part, I have secreted upon me a landing device invented by Kate Howe and manufactured by me. I'll need it, I'm certain; and it may be that I have after many, many years, at last stumbled upon a way around Richard's policy forbidding the promotion of my products. Said rule represents an ethical position worthy of Ralph Nader, which Richard enforces with Stalinist vigor.

Now, How to Dress for Arrest.

There's no objection to the Urban Angler look I've carefully selected to take this fall and winter: jeans, and boots without laces to hang from. Val has a shirt at ready, this long-sleeved, full-cut number, blowzy but with good drape, a deep rust color hearkening back to Nature's own palette—so unlike the diaphanous shirts of last trout season, all mauve and taupe and oleander, which this year we realize were simply clingy *nouvelle*, "bodice bursters" with less subtlety than leather stirrups and stiletto heels—may they never return.

"Looks good," says Val.

"I don't know," murmurs Richard. "In black-and-white, it'll show gray."

Val shakes his head. "I'm telling you, we're going to get one of those fish. This will be a color cover shot. Somewhere."

"What do you mean by that?" demands Rich.

"See what else I've got."

Richard likes a pale one better—a shade of peach that would show white, but so sheer I'm too humiliated to speak. Worse yet, it has all those mysterious loops and button-tab-somethings that baffle fly fishers, but which might come in handy down the hill, at some bar in The Castro.

"Local color," Rich says slyly.

Rust it is, but the Great Hat Controversy lasts almost ten minutes. I end up sampling my way down the length of Val's wall, where hang his specimens; then returning to the first. Rich and Val each suggest the other has no *real* understanding of baseball caps, but it's only tension, the kind of high-wire hum paratroopers feel as the plane begins to climb.

Richard's Jeep, a black kidney-breaker, brings back fond memories. For example, on the smoothest of roads, the brutal suspension reminds me of a dry freestone streamed I drove down when racing to fight a forest fire in the Kaibab.

I don't remember so many commuters on that trip, though we've waited for the worst of traffic to settle. Even after fourteen lights in six blocks, the first view of the pond surprises us. There's the water—and there's the tree-cutting crew not 100 yards away, two guys in orange vests. They are leaving even as we pass, but their presence seems ominous.

So does the layout. From the road it's obvious that both north and south banks are distressingly exposed, visible to, like, fifty cars a minute. But those are the choices: the east and west ends of the pond—perhaps it's three acres in all—are dense with brush, choked down to the water.

We park, make our way down the path. As we walk Val and Rich discuss where Rich will stand on the slope opposite, and the code he will call to signal when he sees danger. It's a dog-walking ruse: "Here, Val! Here, boy! Here, Val-Val-Val!" Nobody mentions that we've forgotten to bring a leash in an area where one is certainly required. Presumably, Richard is walking his cat.

Thirty feet from the bank Val stops suddenly. "It's changed," he says. "It's really changed." In fact, what he had described as clear water, or at least the clearest pond of any in the park, now floats rafts of algae. In places the stuff is as thick-looking as lily pads. It's especially heavy near a small tree that Val had hoped would provide a modicum of cover. The only open water nearby lies just below a steep hillside.

"It doesn't look good," Val says.

On the other hand, for shooting pictures the setting is perfect. A towering tree, tall as any this side of the redwoods, rises up from a wild thicket of vines, blackberry brambles, and wet hummocks of high grass. The sun has burned through the early morning clouds, so we're washed in light both brilliant and soft, reflecting green everywhere, light shades of new leaves mingling with the dark survivors of winter. The pond mirrors it all from where we stand, smooth and emerald, distinct from the color of land around it only for the addition of a cool, slate gray. Distinct also for a rise forty feet out, a take so pronounced and deliberate that a ring of water swells out from a sink-sized depression left in the surface where a large body has pulled down. . . .

"Right here," I say. I am already setting up the rod.

Val laughs. "What did I tell you? But it might be safer if . . ."

"Why don't we try here," says Richard, double-timing toward his station, cat-less, leaving us to the carp.

Which are there. We see a small school moving now, twenty feet offshore—dark, heavy fish, save for one of the biggest, which is a kind of smokey gold with gleaming scales etched at the edges by black. I count four, then six—not as many as I expected. They move with slow certainty that looks somehow luxurious, like creatures of leisure swimming a constitutional on some aquatic promenade.

"What's this?" asks Val, I turn to see him lifting a tangle of heavy monofiliment. "Is this yours?"

I shake my head, convinced immediately that the game has changed. The English say that few carp are caught twice. And that they learn by watching.

I kneel, work out line. The little rod is parabolic and flexes all the way to my hand. The fish travel past us, right to left, paralleling the bank. I cast well ahead, watch intently. Even from above they look fat. By the occasional hesitation or effortless tilt I am convinced they are feeding, but at the pace of diners already satiated and now selecting dinner mints. One lifts his head to my crust of deer hair. Not two inches away, he shifts to one side, slides by.

Time to check the pulse.

"Val! Val! Here, Val!"

"Derelict" really does describe a man who takes drink beyond a point, and this one seems utterly absorbed as he hikes behind us, down the bank, to take his seat at the bench near the small tree Val coveted. The man's mostly hidden from me by branches, but I have the sense his stare is set, that he's unlikely to see us or to care a whit if he does.

I roll-cast again to fish we see cruising. Four times, five. No response. I dare a longer reach; nothing.

"Boy, I thought they'd be right on it," says Val.

It takes me a minute to tie on a dropper the color of algae. "Take your time," he adds, fiddling with his Nikon. Sure I will, though by now we've been observed by a thousand or two cars, many of which are that brand of expensive German sedan preferred by autocrats with cell phones. Just the kind of twits who call in minor infractions even as they slaughter pedestrians in crosswalks.

First cast with the dropper I see a fish of four pounds track the nymph's descent, accelerate toward it, then turn away faster than he'd come.

"Judas Priest."

"You know," Val says, "I think they might be smarter than I thought."

"They've been fished for."

"Maybe so. Looks like it."

Another refusal. My right knee aches. The nymph sinks the deer-crust. I knew that hair was too fine for spinning, but didn't think it would need to float so long. When both flies disappear from view I balance the little rod in my palm, as if to hair-set a trigger. But carp can mouth a bait without moving line; and a fly won't long stand the inspection of those lips. Val shoots a photo.

"Val! Here, Val! Val!"

We see the man, and he us. Later Richard will say that he might have worn an orange vest, but from our perspective it looks like a shirt in not quite the official color. Certainly he's studying us intently, from directly across the pond, perhaps 300 feet away.

I've been holding the rod below the tops of some high grass in front of me, trying to offer no silhouette. But what, pray tell, can we pretend to be doing?

"Touch me, Val. Touch me there."

"What?"

Nah, I don't even think of that ruse for a week. But it's the one that might have worked.

"Don't worry about him," says Val.

I'm not, much. I'm too worried about these fish. I watch a fifth or sixth approach another cast, veer away at just inches.

It's got to be smell.

"You know," says Val, "Hal Janssen says smokers should mask their scent."

For years I rinsed my hands in vinegar before I fished. Could be nicotine, or another chemical in my skin. Might even be the deer hair.

Val chooses and ties on the next fly of the dozen I've brought, this one an orange Glo-Bug pattern. Carp are infamous for eating other species' eggs, which is one reason they've lost our love.

There's exactly one fish visible by the time we're ready. It's a big dark beast, a solitary brute, heading right, this time.

"Here, Val! Here, Val!"

Richard has edged down the hill and, from behind the cover of a shrub, points toward the orange watcher. Val waves and nods, not the least bit catlike. I let the Glo-Bug soak a moment, cast, watch it slowly drift down. The carp continues toward it. He looks to turn, but suddenly I lose sight of him in the tall tree's reflection; so I am watching the fly when the black back appears a yard behind it, closing with supreme confidence. The head angles down.

I strike by sight.

"Got 'im."

"You got one?"

"Yes."

I actually see the fish lift his head as if to test the tension even as I flip clear a coil of line which falls toward the water and then snaps up toward the stripping guide. A dozen more feet whisper through my fingers until I'm on the reel, which spins nearly silent, because for three hundred dollars you don't get a damn drag.

Val has dropped down. The camera clicks. "Hold the rod up," he says, because I have laid it nearly parallel to the ground, pulling left even as I surrender sixty feet to the run. I lift to vertical for an instant—Val shoots—then I drop down again, marveling at a flex now deep as a longbow. Val shoots, says something, shoots. Then, "I'm through the roll. I'm changing film."

My turn to reassure. "Take your time. This will be a while."

Odds are. I'm nearly to backing. The line slicing the surface spooks a school of fish way out. Forty feet beyond that a trio of coots flees a disturbance just beneath them.

"Is he big? Is he strong?" Val's voice is urgent and happy. His face is once again hidden by the camera.

"Big. Very strong."

"Wonderful. Hold that position . . . great. Again. Now how's he fighting?"

I almost laugh, but just then the fish changes direction, rushing toward our bank at an oblique angle, heading for a spot where tree branches trail into the water. For the first time I bear down on the rim and test the tippet.

"Raise your rod. Raise the rod."

"Wait a second."

The fish swirls, doubles back.

"Good. That's great. How big is he?

"One of the big ones."

"That's so great. Man."

"Here, Val! Here, Val!"

"Forget that! Never mind—watch the fish!"

I do, seeing Val creep closer at the periphery of my vision. Then the fish turns to swim directly at us and I am stripping fast, the rod pulsing with each pull of my arm.

At twenty feet we get a glimpse of him. At ten he sees us. I swear I see his eye roll; the rod arcs sharply down. Just as the last loose line is again snapping toward the spool a loop wraps around the reel handle, but the rod's soft action surrenders so much I get a moment of mercy—and back on the spool.

"How big is he?" Val asks softly. "How much do you think he weighs?"

Carp have always seemed to me a little light for their size. "Six pounds. Or maybe eight."

"He's much darker than I thought."

At the end of this run the rod tip rises half a foot, as the fish reluctantly lifts his head. It won't be long now.

I crab-walk to the edge of the water. The soil looks like soft mud, but Val's already checked and found it slick hardpack. I grind in a boot heel. With my left hand I remove a mesh bag from my pocket, slip my hand through the mouth, stretch to feel tension from a lanyard tethered to my waist. A carp may not be as slippery as a bonefish, but close enough. I'll need to hold this one up for a picture and he's so broad I won't find a decent grip anywhere but at his tail.

Four minutes and two runs later that proves true. And even his tail is thicker than my wrist. I have it, all right, but three times my other hand slips from beneath his head—I'm trying not to touch his gills. Irony: where I grew up, regulations required anglers to kill all carp caught.

At last he settles. Val rinses his face—the fish's—and begins shooting over and over. With hat, without. Looking at camera, looking at carp. Val is completely absorbed, engaged, focused more closely than his lens. His directions are quick and excited. Once I look away to check on the orange man—he's gone! and soon, also, our right to vote!—but Val orders my head around. "Don't worry about it, never mind, this is great. I just hope the fish isn't too dark and can't you smile any better than that?"

It's the streaked beard—I knew it.

"Tilt his belly up." I do. Carp have mobile eyes and one of his is watching mine. Lacking any other expressive feature, he appears calm, and even seems to rest. Suddenly I wonder if fermentation has already begun—if he's already *drunk*.

"Cheers. To the musketeers of the magnificent Carp-capade."

We raise aperitif glasses, because Val has only an ancient bottle of Grand Marnier in his cabinet, just enough. We're posing on his deck in front of moose antlers. The timer goes off, with flash. "I want to go back," says Val firmly. In fact, before we'd even trotted up to the Jeep with the deed done and recorded, Val was glancing back over his shoulder. "This is crazy. Crazy."

Of course.

"I mean, how can we leave all those fish?"

Richard laughed then and laughs now.

"You know, it really was easier than I thought," Val continues. "Not the fish—they were harder. They had me worried. But you know, the mechanics of it all."

"Face it, we're good criminals," Rich declares. He hasn't yet mentioned his disappointment, that there's no shot of cops folding me into a squad car, no grainy black-and-white of my face above an ID plate or divided by bars.

"How did he fight again?" asks Val.

"Like a brown trout, but maybe longer."

"He wasn't actually long, though. Just heavy. Really deep."

"Big fish," says Rich.

"And get this: I've got to jog by them tomorrow, look down, and know what I'm missing." Val is clearly dismayed. "That doesn't seem possible. Does it?"

I'm remembering how the little rod flexed in my hand, wondering if I could have actually seen a curve in the cork grip. I do like that rod.

"We can always go back," says Richard. "And if we didn't get a decent shot, we'll have to."

Val shakes his head. "We got the shot. I know it."

He looks wistful for another moment, then brightens. So does Rich, looking over his glass.

"We don't need an excuse," says Val.

"We know where they are," says Rich.

"And that they will take a fly."

After a week, the memories remain. And in the end, perhaps it's not the carp that is most remarkable, miracle fish though it might be. Maybe there's another magic to consider, however modest:

Among the three of us, we have well over a hundred years of angling experience. With Val leading the way, naturally, we've fished something like thirty states, including Alaska; add Canada, Mexico, Belize, the Bahamas, Christmas Island, New Zealand, Polynesia, Southeast Asia, many parts of Europe—every continent but Antarctica. We've landed several-score species of freshwater fish, somewhat fewer, but still lots, from the salt. We make part or all of our livings from the business end of the sport, read what must total 100,000 pages a year, examine a whole bunch of pictures.

Yes, it's obvious where I'm going—to the idea that we could still thrill to a dandy adventure of stealing off to catch carp. Of course, we compounded the thrill by exaggerating fears of a fine we could have easily paid, or Richard could, and embarrassment we would have survived and probably bragged about. Which doesn't suggest that our morning needs to mean any more than this: when it comes to passions that provide pleasure, however esoteric, odd or slimy,

Carpe diem, carpe carp.

Carpe that sucker by the tail.

9

Carpe Diem 256

I head back to the truck, trudging along in that loose happy way I get after eight hours in a float tube when I am chilled in every extremity, including a few favorites which have fled up into a body cavity where they will be that much closer to the warm coffee I shall soon consume.

I know what comes next, so I fumble about in my memory of the day. In this mixed-bag impoundment I've taken some big rainbows and, often in pairs on point and dropper fly, one billion small bass. I found the trout along deepwater drop-offs, in channels between tall weed beds dying in winter. The bass babies were everywhere, obviously, darting out from shreds of cover, five inches long and quick as bats.

Leo is already ensconced in the driver's seat drinking something steamy. "How'd you do?"

Jeff has folded himself in back. "Let me guess," he says, then waits for me to answer.

I grunt. They really are two of the nicest guys you can find to fish with—funny, thoughtful, generous and genuine. Leo's the kind of fellow whose character is widely described as "sterling"; clean-cut as a diamond, a neatnik, he grins at my slobbery as if thrilling to evidence of an unusual life form—"The Miwoks called them 'Wakadoo,' which means 'Fisher Who Creates Great Chaos.' " As to Jeff, well, after a decade of marriage his wife, Lisa, still eyes him with kindly admiration and has asked me at auctions, "So what kind of new rod do you think Jeff would *really* like?" Their son, Josh, approaches an impossible age; even *he* likes Jeff.

Terrific fishing partners, no kidding. Only . . .

They count.

I don't. But I still have to answer. "Between sixty-five and eighty fish," I say. Then, airily, and with a teensy wave of one hand, "Of course, some were bass."

They laugh. "Some, I'm sure," Leo observes. Then both wait again for me to fess up.

Can they be fixed?

Can I?

Left alone I rarely count anything. Truly. Of all the kinds of counting in the world, I am not interested in many. I do not balance checkbooks, have only a general idea of how much money I make and once forgot my age for six months, guessing myself a year older. Numbers simply do not enter my head by the same inlet as other information: there's a backup at a toll gate where exact change isn't enough. Three times in adulthood I've had to relearn the multiplication tables.

So then, *not* counting isn't necessarily a moral issue for me, but maybe a perceptual problem related to poorly titrated medication. Perhaps there's also a mock-Zen issue here, since a week before this outing I wrote dialogue for a character I'll name Split Cain, Flinger of Grasshopper, Greased-Line Priest, who gives his fish count thusly: "There is the first, the last, and, most importantly, the next."

"You must have taken fifteen," Leo urges, meaning trout.

"I don't think so. Nine. Or twelve."

"I landed six," says Jeff.

"Seven or eight, then," I say.

"No," says Leo. "How many did you get when you were off in the cove? We couldn't see you."

I look at him, then Jeff. They're both pleasantly attentive.

"Two hundred and fifty-six," I say firmly.

Which is exactly—*exactly*, I tell you—the number I would put on the day, if I must, representing not just a count of every fish, but including a precise score for each one, this determined by factoring in, oh heck, lots of things, adding and subtracting with a vengeance and representing finally an aggregate total *that says it all*. The process is entirely too complex for human understanding, which I will demonstrate after this detour:

Fly fishing is a fine solitary sport as well as one in which partners may play together against a host of natural opponents.

By way of experiencing such grace, read a Haig-Brown rhapsody or a Gierach adventure with A. K. Best. Compare these to a "friendly" striper competition I witnessed in which one party measured his big one against his buddy's, over and over again, laying down these twin dead fish, lineside to lineside, and finally *stepping* on his own, just like the old joke, so that its dead lips pouted out farther. . . .

Why fly fishing in this country is mostly absent of such measures—*mostly, mostly*—is an interesting question.

I think it's because of the complexity of the mysteries mentioned and soon to be cleverly detailed: there are infinite problems to scoring such vastness. In addition, most fly fishers I know angle a realm where quantities assess a tiny part of the experience. It's not that numbers are irrelevant, just too simple—"On a scale of one to ten identify your love for your children, fear of slow death, and the excitement you feel while pursuing a splendid animal alive in the labyrinthine and alien world of water."

Leo and Jeff both know this. Cognizant of a hundred variables, they still search for small ways to measure the skills and knowledge they employed on this day against *what is possible*. The count of another angler may help here, as may formulas, like "There's 2,700 trout per mile here; I got two." It's a clue to an angling *par* most counters seek, rather than a position on a leaderboard, a sense of "How well should I have done?" Along with this usually comes an invitation to share knowledge: if Jeff's five fish averaged 24 inches each and mine only five, if Leo's tactic or fly caught him two brown trout, then an exchange means we each walk away better prepared for next time.

So . . . counting means little, yet can be of value, a blaze on a tree in a forest of factors. At its most banal it says, "I did better or worse than you did." At its most profound it hints at multitudes of other outcomes, drifts not taken, successes and failures that might have been or could be another day.

Given that, Jeff and Leo might well wonder how I got exactly 256. Luckily, I have a three-and-a-half-hour drive during which I may lecture them on eleven of ninety-seven categories I considered. To wit:

Casts per fish: "We caught an eight pounder every two casts," I read in *American Angler* this morning, "fast fishing in anybody's book." Maybe for *them:* if their 4:1 cast-to-fish ratio is worth 100 points, I should easily get a 210 for this day, my billion baby bass putting me way over the top. Naturally I'll subtract points for the low Size-to-Species Mean, since *en masse* my billion-bass mass was only six-point-four pounds. I'll add a Low Water Temperature Bonus, then delete the High Alkalinity Variable and get, of course, 61 points.

Into this figure I'll carefully divide duration of cast, since a damsel-nymph sink-and-crawl can take several minutes, or half an hour if you're drifting in a pram in a breeze. (That's nothing—I know anglers who let midges sit for longer than it takes them to mate and die. The midges, I mean.) Contrast such waits to a three-heartbeat drift through a fastwater pocket.

Which one might have waded rapids to reach. On streams, there's Stalking Time Per Cast to consider, along with Long Studies of Complex Lies, Painful Knee-Creeps to Proper Position, and the awful but highly point-profitable, Walk-on-Tiptoe-in-Deep-Sucking-Mud Approach. Once on the Sac I caught five rainbows without moving my feet; altogether, however, they score lower than a single Yellow Creek brown for which I hiked a mile and cast once.

Never mind that, we've got issues enough on this lake, what with Strikes-Per-Hookup Averages, and Hookups Per Fish Landed. Time Spent Fighting Fish, subtracted from Odds-of-Survival Penalties, even when mitigated by the Best Reviving Bonus, can actually make it a smart tactical move not to fish at all; and a single careless kill can wipe out a week of high totals.

Now let's get complicated: one certainly can't stop before tallying up Tactics Tried and Techniques Applied. I won't, anyway, since I am prone to change styles both if something doesn't work well, and if it works too well too long. Of that bass multitude, for example, no more than seventeen came on the same fly.

Which I tied. From a pattern I modified—that brings up the question of self-reliance, of quandaries identified, enumerated, and resolved. I mean, if somebody hands me all I need on a stick—"Fish a size 18 PT, six feet of 6X on a fifteen-foot leader, green yarn indicator, shake out line on a straight downstream drift"—and I catch twelve trout, that dozen won't beat three for which I had to discern a hatch, tie a fly to match, and try three tactics to fish properly. (Note here: Jeff not only invents his flies, he wraps his rods and carves his staff. Someday he'll knit his own waders, I believe.)

Have we mentioned casts yet? Delicate presentations to rising fish, cruisers whose rhythm we've timed and direction assessed? With a dry fly? With an emerger? Have we added points for fish-wildness, deducted for bent fins, or for trout hooked while trolling and smoking cigarettes? Discussed the near-fatal loss of style points if a fish regurgitates Power Bait into your palm? And talk about your extra credit, how about 4,000 points for a brown trout that disgorges a vole? A *live* vole. . . .

Ah, boy. If fly fishers' statistics appeared on trading cards, they'd have to print each one as big as billboards, or in four-point type.

Leo and Jeff know that. Even though they count. In fact, you'll often hear one or the other of them shift from individual to team scoring. "We took a score between us" will say the guy who took seventeen himself.

The Royal Plural, is what We call that.

Which brings me, at last, to 256.

I took a five-point deduction for that hare-brained bass that ate both flies of a cast, added eighteen bonus points for two hooked-jaw rainbows, then twenty-nine more for a male that snagged honors in the category of

"Best Crimson Stripe with the Sun at My Back." I put in Leo and Jeff for a hundred points each, because I enjoy fishing with them, subtracted 7/32 for them counting; added eleven for the dandy Brassie Jeff gave me, then twelve more for Leo's sly laughter when he offered to stop in Corning on the home to buy anchovy-stuffed olives. An internal umpire insisted that I factor in my afternoon nap, when I nestled in wool as the wind swept my face and rustled through a sea of grass as mallards crossed clouds through a rainbow of light refracted by my eyelashes. *Huge* point loss after that, when sombody's gray hound woke me by snuffling in my ear—offset, happily, when his fur smelled of clean dust and Timothy hay.

What was left was 256. Easy. At least.

10

❧❧❧

The Ummm of Ignorance

❧❧❧

It was a difficult moment for all of us, I believe. I know it was for the blond couple at the fly-shop counter, who had delivered themselves to the store in a new German car which retails for less than Louisiana, the Purchase. Only a minute before they'd seemed so young and brash, grinning through good orthodontic work as "Troy" explained that "Trixie Peaches" (names and hair color may have been changed to protect the innocent, but maybe not) had bought him this cool fly-fishing outfit for Christmas, but he hadn't *quite* mastered casting. "What I'm having trouble with, see, is how you get all the skinny line off the reel, so that you can reach the fat line underneath, which is what you're supposed to throw with, right?"

I know my brows furrowed as I interpreted this; but the shopkeeper looked as if he was entering a fugue state. "Wait a minute," he said. "You wound on the fly line first—the fat stuff—then put the skinny white backing on top of that?"

"Right. Because it's the 'backing.' That part I figured out."

Oh.

"Well," said the shopkeeper. "Well."

I watched him struggle to find a face-saving way to explain how this actually worked. He did a fine job, too; even so, soon the pretty pair turned the color of Glo-Bugs.

I felt their pain. I did. Mine too, since I'd almost bitten through my lower lip in a successful effort to suppress laughter; but also, I mean, imagine the frustration of some poor fellow with a hundred yards of loose Dacron at his feet when he finally reaches the wrong end of a weight-forward line, then starts to waggle his rod back and forth while calling out something like "Okay, I'm going to make one of those fake casts now. . . ."

Been there, done that. Not exactly that, actually, but worse, I'm sure. Memory has a way of losing things. Didn't I once say, not so very long ago, "Oh, you mean caddis, the *insect.*"

As opposed to what? Caddis, my sweet sister? Caddis, the plural pronoun for people who carry golf clubs? Cadiz, a port in Andalusia—suddenly plunked right down here in casual fishing conversation?

Many dim things have I done in my time. More than enough to develop empathy for somebody like Troy, who'd just confessed to the equivalent of trying to start a car by cranking a key in the trunk lock.

Boy, how we hate feeling the fool. Or looking one, anyway. Ignorance is such an embarrassing sin, even in an era when human knowledge—if not understanding— seems to double every decade. According to the results of a recent study conducted entirely in my mind and on the fingertips of one hand, 37 percent of all people (and 93 percent of adolescents, who may become people at a later date) would rather be considered evil than ignorant. For good reason, too: if knowledge is power, what signifies a lack of it? Consider that if your auto mechanic determines you haven't a clue, it's obligatory for him to identify dangerous damage to your transactor manifold auto-miter unit—and the labor alone on that job will kill you. Could even cost as much as a good beginning fly-fishing outfit: 2,600 dollars, I hear.

How does one learn then, and still maintain from the get-go an image all-knowing?

Hmmm.

"Ummm," actually: and you simply must master this most nearly inert of active responses. So forthrightly vague, so manifestly ambiguous and obviously enigmatic: "umm" actually begs interpretation, thereby shifting the risk of making an erroneous assumption—a form of ignorance— onto the party to whom you're talking. For example:

"Under conditions like these," says your expert, "when you will want to imitate gassy *Rhyacophila* emergers, it's better to fish a tight line with light tippet, so consider throwing a Bimini twist into your leader, the better to protect yourself as you execute the Leisenring lift."

Say what?

All you know for sure is that none of those terms appears in the pamphlet that came with the outfit Trixie Peaches laid on you. For a moment you even wonder if you've committed to some kind of rodeo game in which you must lasso flatulent insects, or maybe flowers, while doing an aerobic exercise.

"Helpless, helpless, helpless, helpless," sang Neil Young. But you can do better by replying simply "Ummm."

Note: that's one syllable, not two. Don't go overboard and aim for "ummm-hmmm," or even "ummm ummm." You want the one hum only, which could mean either,

"Heck I always twist a Bimini ahead of my trilobal-nylon-tied LaFontaine Sparkle Pupa, pal," or, just as easily, "Look! I can make my lips vibrate!"

Which is it? The expert, recently so confident, must now study your face for a clue. He who was testing now is tested: "Did he get that? Is he impressed or depressed? And why do his lips vibrate like that?"

What you say next is critical. It may well determine whether the day is fine or a fine waste of time, so don't even make eye contact until you decide on one of the following approaches, the first five of which I strongly recommend against:

Option 1, mentioned here to get a laugh, goes like this: "You know, none of that sounds familiar to me, but if you'll go through it slowly, not only might I catch fish, but I bet I'll learn something." This silly approach is called the "Honest Abe," and is named for a man who was shot in the back of the head.

Option 2, The New Jersey Gambit: "Talk to me like that again, I'll have your rod crushed."

Option 3, adapted from "Mau Maus and the Flak Catchers": "Gee, you really are brilliant about all this. I mean, a guy like you probably knows everything about fish, also plants, probably, even succulents and bulbs. And oh, I bet you look so good in rubber pants."

Option 4, The Arch Ignorant: "Do any of your people speak English? Don't get me wrong; I love the way y'all wade."

Option 5, The Caustic Angler: "If I knew how to do all that, would I need your sorry ass?"

I hope you can see the problems inherent in these; yet people try. Instead, consider the following, which all begin with "Ummm," followed by a knowing smile:

Option 6, Stranger on Strange Water: "Not being certain am I how we are calling these things in my country, but perhaps is wak-a-nuni, wak-i-ra? You to show, please?"

Option 7, The Sympathy Play: "Man, I probably knew that stuff before my accident."

Option 8, For Your Life, Teach Me: "Now see, I would know all that f— sh—, if I hadn't spent all those f— years in Atascadero, trumped up bull— charges, like I would ever use a f—ing serrated blade, you know what I'm saying?"

Option 9, So Blue My Blood: "I am sorry. I only fish dry flies. Upstream. To rising fish. In England."

Option 10, Enough About Me: "We'll get to all that, but first, how long have your corneas been that color, and can you describe how it feels to pass fluids?"

"Not bad," you probably said to one or two of the above. But remember that saving face is only the half of it. The real challenge is how to get good teaching and, simultaneously, present yourself as all-knowing.

Impossible?

Yeah, just about. I mean, you can stretch it a time or two, as in, "It so happens that I've been doing a study of how experts fish gassy emergers on 7X, so before I jump in here and contaminate the experiment, perhaps you could first show me your methods. . . ." Immediately or eventually, however, somebody's going to suspect you. What happens then?

Ummm. . . .

Probably nothing. Unless you're pretentious, and the real expert has that reason or another for putting you in your place; and I suppose you could be in trouble if your expert is also an orifice, eager to indulge the sort of self-aggrandizing one-upmanship that ultimately leads to a lonely death.

But usually, nothing happens. Nothing bad, anyway. Maybe because most people are mainly sympathetic, aware of how often, in a complicated world, each of us will wade too deep, knowingly or not. You might even be surprised by how many folks are willing to acknowledge their own vulnerability, or at least suggest that in the way they handle your fopah, which is spelled differently. Notice the linguistic pirouettes in the response here:

"So, I guess this isn't a *Callibaetis* nymph after all?" says the enthusiastic novice, after you've examined his precious specimen.

"Actually, in this part of California we call that a 'crayfish,' or 'crawdad.' But you know, it's the same color as some *Callibaetis*, and, absent the claws and tail, nearly the same shape. So even if this crayfish is, like, nine or ten thousand times larger than a mayfly, if you were seeing it at a great distance. . . ."

Nice, eh? But it can get better. A few folks will even attempt a variation on the rare and wonderful "Eleanor Roosevelt Maneuver," demonstrated by a First Lady who defines First Class. Went something like this: at a large and elegant White House dinner, guests were provided finger bowls. A newly popular ingenue, unfamiliar with the protocol, presumed her bowl held water for drinking, so proceeded to do just that.

Everybody noticed. The titters began. This would hit the society page. Scratch one up-and-comer from the wrong side of some tracks, or at least reserve her a place beside The Babe when he's describing what asparagus does to his urine.

But no! Hostess Eleanor Roosevelt, recognizing impending disaster, offers to her guest a gracious smile, raises her finger bowl . . .

And drinks.

Which brings me back at last to our scarlet Troy, Trixie Peaches, and a bemused shopkeeper.

The last slowly began to nod. "Backing goes on the *back* of the line," he said evenly. "It does make sense. It's a common enough mistake, I imagine." Then he looked right at me.

"Ummm," I replied.

"You did it too?" Troy asked hopefully.

"A-a-a-ummm," I managed, breaking the single-syllable rule with enough emphasis that my sinuses rattled. "Ummm, it's hard to remember one mistake in so many, beginning, really, with Adlai Stevenson. . . ."

Long pause.

"You didn't, did you?"

"Ummm."

There followed another brief silence, then four people began, gently, to laugh.

Which ain't all that bad.

11

White Ducks and Hula Poppers

For me it began at about the age of ten, when I was old enough to walk a mile home alone from school. Right outside the recess yard of Madison #2, over the fence behind the high-jump pit, after a quick scoot along the third fairway—

Into the weeping willow. If I'd been spotted on the way in I'd see the golf pro zipping from the clubhouse on his Cushman, leaning forward as if to lead with a forehead that blazed wonderfully red. If my Grandpa Charlie had apple carts and fishmongers for sport in Harlem, as I was told, by God I had this pro and his Cushman, at Town & Country Golf, in Phoenix, Arizona.

More often than not, however, I'd slip in undetected, one of few life forms that moved so urgently in the heat of a desert afternoon, under the buzzing whine of a vast cicada chorus. Handline time at the pond . . . soon the bluegills would school around me as my bread baits dissolved, only to scatter when a bass moved in.

I did get caught. Often, I got caught, after an hour or so. Some golfer would tattle, alerted by my feral manner, or by an image of his Titleist lodged in my brainpan. Then the pro would race over to rag me, voice rising almost to a shout, his forehead shining bright.

That's where I would focus while standing at attention and staring at the reddest spot—about three inches above his nose—all the while nodding emphatically, and answering, "Sir, yes sir!" as he swore for the fifth, eighth, and twenty-sixth time, "*Next* time, I'm gonna call the cops!"

"Sir, yes sir!"

"But there won't be a next time, will there, boy?"

"No *sir*."

"Dammit! That's what you said last time!"

"Yes sir! I remember that, sir!"

I was a trial for him, I really was. Fate had led him to a cushy job on an executive golf course with a pond destined to be fished by me—a temptation I could no more resist than ripe summer mulberries or the fat horned toads I found sunbathing on the slopes of Squaw Peak. One of life's absolutes: the course had a pond, so I would come, and the pro—*my* pro, I eventually considered him—would howl at the gods.

What made this affair special, I think—that is, especially frustrating for the poor man—were my relentless good manners. Surely I was the most polite of nuisances, sincere, agreeable, if not quite remorseful. An ex-military type, he seemed ever baffled by a defiance that was evident only in my actions, never in attitude or words. I was determined, but *sympathetic*, genuinely sorry that it was him I had to trouble.

Had to. As in, "Boy, do you know how *much* it pisses me off to keep finding you here?"

"Yes sir, I do. Honest. I really believe I do know that. Sir."

"You do . . . Well then *why do you do it?* Why? Can you tell me that?"

"I can't help myself, sir."

"You can!"

"No, sir. It's the fish. They're here, so I have to catch them. Where else can I find them?"

"Anyplace!"

"Where? Because I really have to catch them, sir. Do you think it might be a disease? Sir?"

"Do I—what?"

"Because my mother isn't sure. . . ."

"No! I don't want to hear about it! Your problem is . . . this isn't my problem!"

Oh, but I was. Reflecting on that fact, I wonder that the man never did seem to grasp the nature of an obsession that still drives me. I suppose he considered me slightly mad; or he did until, with one daring move, I turned diabolical.

Neither of us could believe it: I initiated a new era of confrontation by walking right through the front clubhouse door, early in the autumn of my sixth-grade year. I'd never actually entered from that direction and for a moment or two I don't believe he recognized me.

Then he did. "What is this?" he said warily, already beginning to crouch slightly. "What are you doing here?"

"Science, sir," I said politely, then passed him an envelope. Inside was a note from Mr. Simpson, my homeroom teacher, explaining my mission. I watched my pro's forehead as he read: "Dear Town & Country Golf Course: Please allow our student to catch specimens of fish for his Science Fair Project. . . ."

" 'Gamefish of Arizona,' " I chirped helpfully. "Mr. Simpson okayed it himself." Sure he did; the proverbial innocent bystander, Simpson couldn't care less if I wanted to collect local fauna.

"For science, sir," I added, always eager to help.

Red right into the hair, was my pro—pink through the cheeks, faintly purple along the nose—this was spectacular. I actually thought a couple of the veins in his temple were going to burst. What was compounding his dilemma, I knew, was that for years he'd been soliciting the school's help in preventing student trespasses, many of which were mine. How would it look now, if he rejected this small favor?

I watched him close his eyes. When he opened them again, they were bloodshot.

"Science Fair project," he whispered. "Oh. Right."

"Mr. Simpson says all the world is a laboratory, sir. He's pretty much convinced of that."

"*Christ* . . . How long is this gonna take?"

Two years, about. Toward the end of the second he started getting cranky again, threatening to call the school, the cops, the parents who I'd almost convinced him had abandoned me at birth, since they never answered the phone at the number I gave him. It was just about that time, however, that I actually started playing golf, kicking in my fifty-cent greens fees and whacking a round before I retreated to the weeping willow to rig up. "Greens fees only pay for golfing here, you know," he cautioned me once.

"Yes sir," I answered, thinking, *Which means the fishing is free.*

And so it stayed well into high school, when I started fishing there at night, jumping the fence, then dodging my way to the pond through the spray of Rain Birds. Sometimes I brought my friend Terry who, after an hour or two, would start eyeing the white ducks. "Look at 'em, buddy, so dumb, so trusting—utterly worthless creatures until they're deep-sixed in my Mom's Coke sauce. What kind of problem do you have with that?"

The trust of my pro, if one could call it that. Then there were the groundskeepers, though during our first encounter I noticed that they looked as wary of me as I was of them. Illegals, I guessed, who lived in the equipment shed among the tractors, emerging late at night. They were always pleasantly surprised when I brought them a soft drink or beer.

By that time I'd long since graduated from handlines, and was either baiting up a spinning rig for the big carp some dunce had introduced into the pond, or throwing a black fly-rod Hula Popper for bass. There weren't too many of these, but some were frightening: once Terry and I spent five minutes babbling after a brute hit a popper with such violence he hurled it four feet up a sloped bank. *"Did you see that!"* we said twenty-four times, varying the accent on each word, then on pairs of words: "Did *you*, see *that? Did* you *see* that?"

Those were the days; and over years, I did spread out my golf-course adventuring. The Encanto Country Club had not only big carp, but turtles of terrible size; and at Papago you could work bass, though it was better, if far more dangerous, to sneak into the Phoenix Zoo ponds nearby. I also fished the Grand Canal where it traversed the grounds of a vast luxury hotel, diving in whenever excited security guards arrived—in Cushmans, again. Often they would putt alongside me as I drifted, shouting and waving their cans of Mace. I don't believe I was quite so polite to them: unlike my pro, they had no legitimate jurisdiction over the water. I knew that, and how to use my middle finger.

* * *

College, after that, some traveling. It was almost four years before I finally found another golf-course pond I could fish with permission, more or less, this time at the Valley Country Club outside Denver, where I was tending bar. I caught stringers of crappies for old Charlie, another barkeep there, along with sunfish and juvenile walleyes; and the bass that surprised my little streamer remains a personal best.

There have been others. Even so, and despite the fact that Town & Country has long been buried beneath condominium complexes, my pro retired, it remains my home course, and a home water, of sorts, first in my memories. I took so much pleasure on the banks beside the ninth hole, and took Melissa there also, on the date when she caught a channel catfish Terry would declare "The best fish I ever ate, though still not a duck." As I recall that evening, she revealed to me a new angle on life, another passion to consider, which we celebrated in the soft rough of Bermuda grass behind the green.

The Rain Birds came on just when you would expect they might. All that was missing in that moment was the whine of a Cushman, and the sight of a red forehead racing down the fairway.

12

Pariah
(No, *You* Decide)

Late one winter, I followed the Truckee River into Nevada—the trophy-trout stretch. The day was bright and cool and so were the fish. A local veteran lamented the drought, then cited studies revealing the river's decline. "Shot to hell. Still, it's good to get out on a day like today."

Miles upstream I waded onto private, unposted land. An owner advised me of my fault, accepted an apology, then offered one of his own: "I mean, I don't *care*—I don't fish—it's just all the garbage, you know? Look at this shore. I cleaned up here last week. Christ, we have to hire kids to do it in the summer." A sad story no longer new. Then, after a little more conversation, "Listen, with you in the water like that . . . the truth is, I can't really ask you to leave."

I didn't, so became unwilling witness to a confrontation down the creek, when the owner politely approached

117

a father and son. "Fuck you," I heard. "Fuck you, mother-fucker."

In front of his son. I filled my vest and arms with litter when I waded my way out.

Above Reno the Truckee's no longer a freestone stream and the sloughs through which it moves are murder to access. I think I smelled brown trout before I gave up.

To Pyramid Lake, late: they were yanking out the doorstop when I drove up to the Indian store where you buy permits. The clerk would answer no questions—"Jus' fill out the form." His reservation, it's true, but I had my own as I paid Caesar his coin, doubts I quickly dismissed. "Got the last ticket sold today," I observed to myself, imagining all the folks already out on the lake, lined up on ladders to double-haul long rods for cruising Lahontans. Trout dinosaurs, these cutthroats, leftovers from a sea that once covered 10,000 square miles; left over also is Pyramid, along with lakes Tahoe and Walker—puddles, comparatively speaking, however vast they seem.

Vast indeed, when you're the only person on one of these. "Got the *only* ticket sold today," I decided, gazing about the moonscape, searching for the glimmer of another light. I did, however, have a billion stars to watch, and for that felt happier than I deserved. By their light I walked the shore, renamed the lake "Sea of Meander," and countenanced no objections.

Back at Viola's front door I found a perfect, unlit Marlboro cigarette. I added chili to Tabasco, inhaled that, then invited Jim Beam to a drink as I sinned with nicotine for the first time in years. Lovely night.

And it was a lovely Lahontan I took the next morning, long and slender, crimson at the gills. I'm afraid it's true that they can be dogs: two short runs and this fish came limp to my hand. "A little relaxed, aren't we?" I inquired. "Practically cavalier? I'm not obliged to fish catch-and-release here, you know." But I did, liberating him to enjoy his leisure.

My hands were numb by then—the wind was coming up, rushing past in great gusts of dry, icy air that burned my skin. I retreated to Viola, who stood her ground, shuddering; but her heater failed. By then I was longing for a little green anyway, so the order of the day was to drive.

Back to 395, into California, north now, just to see what was there. At a roadside market I stopped for soda and gasoline, and to check their dusty rack of sunglasses. Don't ask me why, but it's always at such places you still find polarized glass, in good nylon frames that don't make you look like a bug. Not this time. "Any fishing?" I asked the round counter woman.

"Oh my word, *yes*," she exclaimed. "They're catching them like mad over at Lake—."

High desert, a low pass, snow banks, evergreens, a bigger town. I stopped for flies and information at a shop not far from the lake. "They are catching them," this new counter woman said thinly. "Quite a few." Then, after a delicate pause, "Do you mind if I ask just *how* you found out?"

What's this? I made a vague reply, then diverted her with a question of my own, about where a man might get his propane heater fixed this afternoon.

Small, neat, pre-fabricated house, tidy brown lawn, a sign that read "Appliances Fixed Here." I had trouble inviting the man down from his porch, though he lit a Marlboro. "Look," he said slowly, "maybe I could get it right, but I'd have to pull it first. That'd take me two damn hours: I'd have to charge you for 'em. Then charge you to fix it. More, to put it back. You see what I'm sayin'."

I didn't quite—or knew I was missing something. "Right. And about how cold was it here last night?"

He inhaled several lungfulls of smoke in lieu of a reply. "Uh-huh. You know, I shouldn't say this, but in a little rig like that, you might as well leave the stove burner on all night. Keep you warm enough, and it's pretty safe if you keep a window open."

I supposed so, then endured another pause, longer but less delicate than that allowed by the store woman. "So," he said suddenly, "I guess you're here for the slaughter."

"How's that?" What was *up* with these people?

He shook his head. "Slaughter. That's all it is. You can call it fishing if you want to."

"Call *what* fishing?" I said, no longer hiding my annoyance.

He shook his head. "Every damn spring. Stupid fish schooling up at the inlet, milling around thick as logs in a woodpile." My heater might not work, but this fellow had one warming his voice. "Ought to be illegal, that's what I say. And if you don't know about it, then how'd you happen to come here?"

I gave a longer explanation than his tone encouraged; I wanted to understand this. He nodded curtly to "catch-and-release," though I don't think he practices same. When I'd finished describing my pilgrim's progress his anger remained, but I was no longer the target.

"Go on out there, you ought to. Take a look for yourself. See all the people filling freezers. It's an immoral shame, I say. But see for yourself; you decide."

A lake of long arms, small coves, and tall trees. The day-use pullout was banked by snowdrifts eight feet high and crowded with cars. From the path I could see a couple of miles of shoreline, all abandoned save for both sides of a narrow bay at an inlet 100 feet wide. Along that bank it was nearly wall-to-wall people—not Pacifica Pier, exactly, but pretty close, with couples and oldsters on lawn chairs in the snow, surrounded by bright bottles of Power Bait, cans of Bud and Coors, and kids sporting Zebcos and neon ski jackets. All the colors of a beach scene without the flesh tones.

No thanks, I thought, then rigged my Buck's Bag and a split-cane rod I had found at a garage sale and had long wanted to fish.

I contemplated sledding down to the water in my tube, but decorum prevailed, so I launched from the point and finned away from the crowd, feeling a little disdainful. Is that fishing? Shouldn't someone be serving Velveeta hors d'oeuvres?

I drifted in a wind, worked the heavy rod. My gloved hands muffled the grip; even so, with every cast the cane came alive—a parabolic action that seemed to spring from the tip-top right down through my wrist, then race clear up into my shoulder. The feel reminded me of a hickory bow I shot as a boy—pull, hold, release, *thisssst*.

The fly was wrong, and the line. I had no clue as to the right change for the first; and I didn't have a full sinker that would load the big rod. For an hour, however, I remained fascinated by its action, my concentration broken only—and often—by triumphant cries from the cove. The wind, a current, and curiosity slowly moved me that way.

Along an invisible line across the cove mouth fish began to boil. Not one had I seen elsewhere; now there seemed to be hundreds. The shore anglers eyed me warily, shot out casts to stake claims. I honored these, fished hard a few minutes, kicked over to land. Three or four fishers were leaving from a spot near the inlet, so I traded fins for flats boots, then waded out from where they'd stood. It was now late afternoon, and the crowd had dwindled to a score. Sound carried; they'd been listening for hours to each other's conversations.

About the time the water reached my knees I began to see trout—two, three, half a dozen. Stockers, they looked like, but their mission was clear: to swim up this too-tiny tributary and spawn. Daring creatures, they would surge into the shallows, watch me, veer off suddenly, then circle back so close I could see their stubby dorsals and the too-silver sides of Purina-fed fish.

The most awkward fisherman of the bunch, a Persian, by his accent, moved in behind and just to the left, immediately beside the mouth of the stream and me. No problem, really—he was throwing a bobber the size of a tangerine, with casts that only averaged eight or ten feet. After each he would let loose with an awkwardly inflected curse. Other anglers glanced at him often, then at each other.

Two late-arriving fly fishermen climbed over the snow and, to my serious annoyance, waded out to bracket me between them. One wore a brace on his casting arm, was friendly, acted as if steelhead protocol prevailed. He asked about my rod, my line, cast three times, hooked a fish, released it, then explained that he has carpal-tunnel syndrome in his wrist "from fly fishing five days a week for three years."

"Nice work if you can get it," I told him, still miffed.

He took no offence. "Yeah, I guess. All it cost me was five back operations and lyin' in body casts for six months after each one. Now I can stand for two hours, rest one, stand two." He looked awfully young for that fate—certainly no older than thirty. "The surgery didn't do jack. But at least it left scars, so people believe me, don't think I'm just a parasite." He turned to me and smiled. "Screwed up my head some, maybe."

Two oldsters took fish simultaneously, then strung these on a wire now thrashing with limits. "Good thing too, George," said one. "Cold's making me stiff." A boy hooked a twelve-incher on his Rooster Tail, forgot to reel, and backed straight up the bank to the cheers of his girl-friend. "Dinner!" he shouted to us. "First one!" she cried. I was reminded that stocked fish are cattle, born and bred for the plate.

Still, I was not at ease. I felt a tension here I did not understand.

The Persian flogged the water and cursed. My back-strained companion turned to glare. I shrugged. "Every-body's got to learn," I said softly.

"That's not it," he answered. "You're supposed to stay fifty feet from the inlet. Fifty feet." Suddenly I understood the knowing glances I'd intercepted.

Now that my companion had said the words to me he seemed compelled to carry on. "Look," he said evenly to the Persian. "You can't stand there. You're supposed to stand fifty feet away from the stream. It's in the regula-tions."

"Fifty feet? Fifty feet? Oh, I am sorry. I din't *know.*" This time the Persian's voice sounded genuine indeed. "*Really,* I din't know." He hastened to move his gear well away—and even paced off the distance, to prove he was earnest.

The tension faded. I actually stuck a fish, then played him slowly on the long rod to enjoy the feel of the cane fibers fighting back. "Soft, isn't it?" said the fly fisherman beside me.

"Soft," I agree.

Just at my feet, the fish twisted off, which didn't bother me a bit. I'd cast the rod and now played a fish, so had a grasp of its nature. That called for a drink, something to warm me from the inside. But I would not get one until a new drama unfolded.

A heavyset man, early middle-aged, lumbered down the snowbank from the day-use parking lot carrying two rods and a pail. He paused a moment, said "Huh," then walked up right to the mouth of inlet, where he set up, baited, and cast.

The Persian looked around. A dozen people kept silent, as they had for him. But the former miscreant—good citizen, now that he knew—spoke up politely. "You know, that someone is not supposed to be there. The regulations are saying you must to stand fifty feet away."

The new arrival looked the Persian over. All bundled up, was the transgressor, though his bald head was bare. "No," he said firmly. "The regs don't say that."

The Persian looked out to my companion. "That's what I heard," he continued uncertainly.

Silence, then the fly fisher beside me turned again. "That *is* what they say. Fifty feet."

Another look-over. "No, they *don't*."

Pause. Beat. "Yeah, they *do*." The fly fisher pointed with his rod tip to the great school of fish we knew circled before us. "You're supposed to give *them* some kind of *chance*."

You could almost hear a growl in the new man's throat and it was hard to say if his head was red from cold or rage. "It's high-water mark," he said. "High-water mark is the law."

"Fifty feet."

"Buddy, I got the regulations in my truck. You want to see them?"

"I don't need to; I've read them. It's fifty feet, mister, that's what it is."

"*It's the high-water mark.*"

The girl of the couple piped up. "I thought it was fifty feet. That's what the lady at the shop told us, I think."

"Fifty feet, she said," added the boyfriend firmly.

I wished intently that I actually knew.

Everybody was silent for quite a long time. When people did speak again, it was softly. We had a pariah on the bank.

He took it as long as he could. Then, in what was almost a shout, "It's high-water mark! I've got the regs in my truck!"

Silence.

"Shit! What does it matter? Look at them—" he pointed out into the water. "Look at 'em—you think they have a chance? In this damn trickle? Look at all *you* people . . . what's right is, that *none* of us should be here! Because every fish in the lake comes into this cove—every damn one! They ought to rope it all off, put up buoys and that kind of crap, make *all* of it off limits! That's the fact! And you all know damn well that I'm right!"

Silence again, but a different kind. Then the pariah threw his rods in his pail and stomped back the way he had come.

Perhaps he went to talk with the appliance-repair man.

I stayed that night in the snowy channel of the day-use parking lot, breaking a rule. Jim Beam came to dinner and dessert, after tipping his cap twice to the carpal-tunnel fisher from whom I bummed two cigarettes. I smoked these late, sending swirls of clouds toward the cracked-open skylight—my ventilation for a stove burner left on. In the shadows of that ring of blue light I traced back my trip, from the declining Truckee trophy stretch to the private water upstream where I took out trash. I'd enjoyed the sky above Pyramid Lake—now "Sea of Meander"—done battle with a doggy dinosaur, then followed a trail of people to a slaughter, if that's what it was. Pleasure and dilemma, questions which, like stars, changed from one color to another, depending on the angle of perception. The pariah at the inlet had been pathetic, but he was right? "*You* decide," I charged back to an image of the angry heater man, then I took solace in a memory of the cane rod flexing beneath my thumb.

At last, I cast into darkness.

13

❧❧❧

Striper Barbie
Does the Bay

❧❧❧

I hit a pattycake backhand, and my groundstrokes threaten traffic on streets not so near the court, but the last time I played tennis my topspin serve still sizzled hairs off the ball. "Last time" is the caveat—1989? 1990, maybe?

The game and I didn't take to each other precisely because of that serve, or the hours that went into learning how, long summer afternoons in the Arizona sun. My father instructed. While baseball was a game for us, a near-daily ritual for a decade, he taught tennis in formal whites, with an eye to a future so distant he overlooked the present. "I don't even want you to swing the racket, just give me twenty-five tosses. No, too low, start over."

It wasn't much fun. It still isn't. So if my daughter, Sophia, wants to whip an old fiberglass rod back and forth at the speed of a bumblebee wing—fast enough that the line makes tiny sine waves rather than loops—so what? If

it pleases her aesthetic to spin seventeen strands of holo-
graphic wing fibers round a size 6 Aberdeen hook, then
palmer a hackle of three twisted marabou plumes . . . hey,
I'll stick a feather on its shank and call it Sophie's Dandy.

And yet . . . I know I must be careful, and sly. There's
a trick to instilling obsession, I'm persuaded, an art to successfully imprinting on children the secret code that will
create our partners for later years. I think it's best to begin
when they're young, then keep the pressure oh-so-light,
like playing a twenty-two-inch brown on a 7X tippet.

Take my tactics with Sophia. Her first Halloween she
went as a golden-stonefly nymph—a "Streetfly," I called
her species, since we live deep in the heart of Oakland,
California.

"That's cool," said my neighbors. "So, like, this Streetfly is some kinda' *roach?*"

"No bugs," Sophie said the next year. It broke my
heart, of course—Lisa had most of a *Hexagenia* outfit already cut out, and I had a gorgeous hellgrammite costume
on the drawing board. But I took it standing up, and
waited until Christmas.

"Barbie fly fishes, you know," I whispered, while com-
posing Santa's list.

"She does?"

"Oh yes. Trout, some salmon, a little saltwater—inshore, mostly. She ties a wicked Clouser. You know, the fly
I said had the Barbie eye."

"*Barbell*, I thought it was."

"Whatever."

"How about Ken?"

"Ken? Oh. Well, he's just a doll; he trolls."

You might be surprised what that led to, though there's
still a fair run to riffle. And I do have reason to hope. Fellow I know named Al Shaw has already come quite a dis-

tance with his son, Robbie. I realized the kid was well-guided the first time I saw him at a sportsmen's show, where he got Lefty Kreh to autograph his cap. Robbie could not have been eleven yet, but Al already had a wallet full of big-fish photos: first rainbow, biggest on a dry fly, that kind of thing. Robbie's also some kind of national yo-yo wizard, which might stand him in good stead if he takes to high-stick nymphing.

He and Sophie are engaged, though they don't know that yet (and she may still entertain hopes about Kenny, heir to Glacier Bay Country Inn). It's not exactly a contract, but I hope to talk Al into folding our funds into a joint college IRA, with part of the proceeds designated for a couples camp at Joan Wulff's casting school.

About then it will be Max's turn. He's my toddler, and his situation is a little bit dicey as yet. There is one stellar prospect: Lauren, Ed Weatherly's daughter, is now tying in shows, even designing patterns, but at the moment she's about six times Max's age. I can only hope she'll go for a younger guy, eventually, if he's as well imprinted as I intend that boy to be.

In fact, I started Max at about six months.

" 'Fish.' See this? 'Fish.' "

"Psk?"

"Right. Fish. Fish fish fish fish fish fish fish. By the way, that lady over there? Call her 'Mommy.' "

Mommy, it so happens, taught Max to purse his mouth at anything with fins, and to make this little plipping sound. It's cute, if a tad too carplike for me.

"Psk," he still says these days, then "plip plip plip."

"That's my boy," I reply, encouragingly. Then, sort of an afterthought—he's almost two now—"And you can start calling me Daddy any day." Meanwhile, the kid's crazy about his crawdad overalls, though he'd better stop pinching the cat.

"You should watch yourself," Lisa warns, with many shakes of her head. "You don't want to end up like one of those obsessed stage moms."

I snicker disdainfully. "Obsessed? Don't be absurd. My kids can fish any stage of insect life they like: nymph, emerger, dun, or spinner. As long as they're happy—that's what counts in life."

She mutters, but I can't be bothered. I've almost got this eight-inch, 8-weight rod wrapped, in threads that color-coordinate with a tiny vest and waders. The rod should throw size 32 poppers no problem, so I think we're all set for Sophie and "Striper Barbie's" first trip on the Bay. Why, even Max has a chance for a fish: he can't cast yet, but I must admit that "Liberace Ken" looks good on the end of his line, tricked out in silver spangles and trailing feather boas, with a 4/0 hook wired to each foot.

14

Angling Through the Looking Glass:

So the Turtle Tortoise

W hat was it I learned in Malaysia, the point of every lesson I remember? Something about the vastness of my ignorance. All these cautionary tales delivered to me with a wink or a slap, and very nearly by strokes of the *rotan* stick—six of which will cripple a man, I was told.

So I was told. Twenty years after the Ministry of Information ended my Peace Corps career I'm still piecing together odd bits of information. Only six months ago, for example, I discovered that the violent fish I knew as the *Ikan keleh* is a stray species of mahseer, once grand prize of British sports in India, famous for crushing hooks between the pharyngeal plates in its throat.

No doubt I'd have made the identification long ago had I not posed all my queries using "Ikan Klee," a spelling derived from Standard English phonetics rather than from the Malaysian language's subtly different usage. In a similar vein, if I'd only asked the children who dogged my River Kangar expeditions to draw the leviathans that twice spooled my largest spinning reel, surely they would have added whiskers along with the terrible teeth they pantomimed, thereby suggesting I tangled with giant catfish, not bull sharks swimming up from the Straits. As for the incident of the Turtle-Which-Wasn't. . . .

But then, seeing one-eyed through the Looking Glass defined my life in Malaysia. Too slowly I learned—or began to understand at a level of mind not easily tutored—that an assumption of my ignorance should be part of my world view, an ontological imperative. So many ways to find trouble: Touch a neighbor with the wrong hand. Laugh at a butterfly. Show the bottom of your foot. Leave out a word that seems obviously redundant. Use certain verbs with emphasis. Ignore an innocent-appearing mix-up of nouns, or accent a second syllable instead of the first. . . .

Like most people who find themselves alien in origin, language, faith, and race, I listened and watched more carefully out of fear that I did not understand what was happening around me. So much goes on between the lines we see; I speculated that I could someday be caught in an enormous cultural current—that I might be lifted like jetsam on an opaque flood rushing toward disaster—and wouldn't even realize that I was wet. Of course, that was part of the adventure, yes? I'd not come so far only to find the familiar all over again. I wanted mysteries of people and place, strange tastes, different gods. I wanted unknown possibilities even in fishing, chances to test my line against a fish that might turn out ten inches long, or ten feet. And if I made mistakes, broke off, committed the odd faux pas, well then, at least I'd try to avoid mortal sins.

I failed at the last, as was indelicately suggested by the Ministry's allegations of Sabotage, Sedition, and Violations of the Internal Security Act. That is not a fishing story, although in the bizarre politics of Malaysia it could easily be confused with one. But angling likely played a role, maybe two, in yet another accusation lodged against me. It also influenced the acquisition of Rashidi as my *adik ankat*—adopted brother—and led me, roundaboutly, to a brutally pragmatic insight into one Chinese soul, which presaged a future that soon would take a wild turn.

First things first: *Mamancing ikan* means "to fish" in Bahasia Malaysia, the standardized language of the country's politically dominant racial group. *Ikan* is actually a classifier applying to fish generally—all fish are *ikan* something or other. "Fishing for fish" seemed unnecessary to me, so in my early meanders through the countryside I would often leave off *ikan* when asking about angling possibilities. "I want to fish," I would say in Malay. "Do you fish? Where? How do you fish? What kind of fish do you like to fish for?"

These questions quite excited some locals, whose responses I could not understand—which should be expected, I reminded myself. Many of the remoter folk rarely met white men, never mind one who spoke a crude version of their "classical" language; imagine the King's English as spoken by a three-year-old with a heavy accent and a smoker's cough. But their reactions made even more sense after I was gently advised that while *mamancing ikan* formally referred to fishing, *mamancing* alone is a vernacular term meaning "to seek sex."

"I want to have sex," was how I'd initiated conversations. "Do you have sex? Where? How do you have sex?" And then, a question which must still puzzle a few Malay

Sons of the Soil, "What kind of fish do you like to have sex with?"

Of course, I can't be certain that these early gaffes led to the local mullah's allegation of *Khalwat*, "Illegal proximity to a woman," the only crime of which I was actually guilty. But I will forever wonder if rumors of my sex-with-fish quest first put them on to me.

Maybe. Or maybe the local mullahs didn't care for fly rods; far more likely is that they failed to distinguish fly fishers from all the other non-Muslim infidels they despised, and so our conflict was inevitable.

So it seemed then. Several times I met patrols of white-robed religious vigilantes, once when returning from the marsh after an evening spent throwing poppers for a frog-hunting bowfin, *ikan haruan*; again, after a night spent working the shoreline below the patio of a Chinese café, where the trash-strewn water reflected strings of colored lights with lotus-petal shades and my fly drifted down like a smaller flower, taken most casts by *ikan yu* built like thick bluegills.

The militiamen merely glowered at me on these two occasions. But the third and last time we met was late one afternoon, when a half-dozen of them swept down to surround me and the small flock of children who converged whenever I drifted prawn baits through runs on the main river. The kids were regulars who mostly liked laughing more than fishing; they often brought me pieces of fruit, or cookies, or just cups of water, then stayed to try out English and giggle at my Malay. Thus would we entertain each other while I waited for anything: cobalt-blue catfish coming through on a spawning run, and weighing from six to twenty pounds; a tiny brown cousin of these with both dorsal and ventral fins which flowed back into the tail, top and bottom, so that the fish looked to have a single, rippling fin wrapped most of the way round; *ikan putih*, carp, appreciated by locals for their pale flesh.

At the mullahs' approach the kids fell silent, which made gratuitous the way several of the men bared teeth behind their beards. I remember that a breeze flapped their robes, giving them the remarkable appearance of enormous white bats. Several carried cudgels.

Fucking bullies. When they were close enough I smiled, inclined my head politely, and asked in English, "So what are you sons of bitches up to today?"

It was a given, in this area, that most orthodox Muslims spoke only Malay, maybe a little Arabic. Even if they'd understood, I don't think they'd have had one ready answer, for in the moments that followed it came clear that this mob was not of one mind. Two of the men clearly wanted trouble, another pair looked like they would play along, if only Allah would specifically promise they wouldn't get hurt; but two more really seemed ready to call it a day, go home to dinner, perhaps snuggle up to a genitally mutilated wife.

The leader, who wore the cap of a Haj, snarled a sentence I didn't understand, except for the phrase *mat salleh*, an argot reference to Anglos which, rated as an ethnic slur, would fall between "colored" and "nigger."

I grinned at that, then nodded vigorously. "Yes," I said, in a tone expressing pleasure that he had recognized me. Then I continued in Malay. "I am Matthew Salleh, but you can call me Matt." With that I touched the butt of the spinning rod to my chest, in a move that happened also to point the tip at the Haj like the sharp end of a bone. "*Chigu* Matt."

Chigu means teacher and it's a word full of status, combining *encik*, "Sir," and "guru." A big deal. "*Chigu* Matt," I repeated deliberately, using the paternal inflection one adopts when inviting a student to repeat a phrase—hey, when you throw a gauntlet, might as well heave the pair. Then I cocked my head inquisitively and shifted over several feet, to put myself between Haj and the children. Smiling into his eyes, I began to slowly roll my shoulders. Just . . . because.

That about did it for the less resolved warriors of God. And I could tell that the bat-pack leader also sensed his troops' uncertainty—save for the rabid enthusiasm from the stick-happy runt on his left, which happened to be his shit-hand side. About then I believe it occurred to Haj that he could soon lose a whole head's-worth of face. I mean, if this *Chigu* Matt managed to dunk a holy man or a few of his party into a conveniently placed river. . . .

In a land where I didn't *faham* much, I still understood the shift in his glare, and had a sense that every threat after that was empty, a salvage effort. I suspected that everybody else felt that too; so I let him rant a little, then we all went home.

Tak mengapa, no problem. Right.

Much to my horror, the next day I looked out from the hotel window and saw several of the kids waiting for me in their customary place by the river, even as they cast furtive glances around them. That worried me, so I took a back way out, using an alley behind the Hindu temple. I waved once to the loosely diapered, incredibly lascivious priest, then slipped downstream through the trees.

The fishing was good but my mood was dark. I quit early because of that, and because of some *Khalwat* I hoped to commit that evening. In my haste I took a shortcut across an oxbow, on a faint path running through an overgrown pasture. The grass was light green and waist high. Some of it bent away from me as I approached.

Cobras. Four-foot monitor lizards and reticulated pythons three times that long—leeches the size of bananas, spiders big around as bread plates, a millipede I taped at fourteen inches: all these I expected to find in this part of the world, and did, eventually. But about tortoises I was never advised. Not even about little ones, much less a fatty almost twenty inches along the back. But recognizing him for what he was gave me a happy moment: first, because he was not a cobra, monitor lizard, or python; then, because I grew up in Arizona, where I sometimes found tortoises in the desert near our house.

Never once did one of those finds kick up the stir that this one did in Kangar. Especially among the local Chinese. A middle-aged man was particularly enthusiastic. "Good tu-tul!" he said in English. "Very good-la!"

"Tortoise, we call this one," I said.

He blinked. "Tu-tul," he replied firmly.

I shook my head, lifted a scaly foot and showed him unwebbed toes. "The land ones, we call tortoise."

He blinked twice. "Tu-tul."

What's this? I wondered. Excepting the orthodox, most Malaysians would avoid confrontation, preferring instead to smile and nod and keep their own council. Not this fellow.

A small mystery compared to another: after serving three fine days as the mascot for our training group, our "Tort-us" disappeared from the back yard of the center where we held classes, despite the fact that we couldn't find any route out he might have managed on his own.

I would have investigated, to be sure. But that afternoon I received a summons to dinner from our training group's "Cultural Advisor." A broad-bodied, Mexican American irrigation engineer, the "CA" was also an ex-Malaysia volunteer widely suspected of harboring secret prejudices, despite his relentlessly politically correct position. All I can report is that he chose to feed at a remote Chinese *kedai* specializing in pork, where he proceeded to order four platefuls of exactly those pig organs we all hope aren't really in hot dogs. He washed these down with ferocious slugs of Anchor beer, and I must note that the pig and hops combination seemed volatile, because each time fumes erupted from his mouth the outburst made a noise that seemed to contain the sound that some claim is the name of the one true God.

Two quarts and many pig nipples, noses, and penises into the meal, he informed me of the *Khalwat* charge, brought, anonymously, to Peace Corps attention.

"But she's not a Muslim," I complained. "And since when are they applying *Khalwat* to the rest of us?"

He shook his head. "Never have before in Perlis State," he admitted. "An' you know, Peace Corps thought real careful about that. Like, 'Hey, wha's fair here, man?' Is this right? Then right after that, I think they just say, 'Who knows, fuck it, les' let them crucify his pink ass, so maybe the Haj will like us better.' "

No cross to bear—only banishment as it turned out, to one of the Malay families who had volunteered to host trainees on "home visits." Of course, before I arrived they probably had little hope of being chosen, being so very far away from Kangar. . . .

Rashidi's father's farm was set well back from any road, deep in a green-on-green plain of jungle, rice *padi*, and rubber orchards, flat land divided suddenly by *bukits*— startling, cliff-sided limestone hills, often so high and thin they look like butcher blades embedded in the earth. A narrow stream separated the house from a forest which must have held every one of Malaysia's forty-two hardwoods; from these trees had been hewn the planking of walls and floors, slabs four inches by sixteen, and forty feet long. Large squares of *padi* spread out from the front of the house, separated one from another by high berms. Off to

the side was a small pasture, grazing for eight or nine cattle, also pens for fifty chickens and three malicious gray
geese.

We were two kilometers south of Thailand, but this
was "East of Eden": Rashidi was the pariah son of a family
that had pirated that classic plot, which they were playing
out with a vengeance. I was made part of that: when
Rashidi was assigned to me in the role of a servant, we
were doomed to furious battle—"the Apache," I called
him—until time and trials taught me that he had a Hopi
soul, wide and generous, with a farmer's love for the lives
he nurtured.

Rashidi deserves a book of his own. It will not enter
any annals of angling, however, though he enjoyed the
dapping we did in the little stream beside the house, where
sometimes we would stand on tree limbs growing out over
the water, poking poles through branches to dangle baits
of rice paste.

That was the first activity one might say we shared.
But it also created another kind of schism altogether, the
day gold and silver broadswords appeared beneath us as we
perched, and for half a minute hacked the water so furi-
ously that desperate fish flew into the air like silver leaves
swept up by an irresistible wind.

It was an assault worthy of barracuda. Big barracuda—
the Atlantic tribe.

Then—like *that*—they were gone.

It took me half a minute. "What . . . was that?
Rashidi . . . *what were those?*"

"Ikan Klee" was how I heard his disgusted grunt. Klee
could not be caught, he said, and weren't worth eating
anyway. Worse yet, the terrified fish surviving in this part
of the stream would not bite for half an hour.

Like I cared about those triflers. I was already obsessed, raking the images left in my mind for shapes barely

apprehended—an eye the size and color of a big English penny, scales like crosshatched armor. Thirty pounds? Fifty?

Rashidi couldn't be bothered. No way. And since this happened before we came to like each other. . . .

Impasse.

Even farmers have a sentimental soft spot or two, as it happens. One of Rashidi's was Buah, a cream-colored bitch of medium size, with eyes more intelligent than any I've seen on one side of the Senate's aisle. The family kept her because of Communist gun runners in the forest; but Rashidi loved her half to death, if always at a distance of more than five or six feet.

And from upwind. "Buah smell so bad-la," Rashidi complained to me, a day after our klee sighting.

I was crabby, distracted, still trying to figure out how to engage his help in catching such a beast. "Yeah. Well, you bathe yourself with your tongue for a week. We'll see how you smell."

"What?"

"So wash her."

"But *orang Muslim*, he cannot to touch . . . the water dog."

"Wet dog," I corrected. "You can't touch her when she's wet. So I hear." Nor could he allow her ever to lick him.

"But *orang* not Muslim . . ."

I saw where he was going and in the same moment an idea struck me like, well, like a ravening klee. "That must be true," I said, wondering how I might finesse this.

"So," he continued, "*you* could to washing Buah."

Slowly, I turned to look at him. Very slowly. On my face was an expression of astonishment bordering on horror. "What?" I breathed.

"Yes?" he said cautiously.

I could only shake my head; I was that overwhelmed. At last I was barely able to whisper . . . "I must."

By then Rashidi was seriously bewildered. He eyed me warily, lips moving as he repeated himself what I had said, by way of considering the translation. Finally, "Must? *Mesti?*"

"Yes."

"Why must?"

Another helpless head shake. "In my country, Rashidi . . . when one man asks another to wash his dog . . . well, there just is no choice. None."

"True?" he said, obviously fascinated.

"Truly."

"So . . . then this very good-la!"

I nodded, hung my head abjectly, then closed my eyes as if in prayer.

"Ha! Then I go get soap!"

"Yes. And also, our fishing rods."

"What? *Apa*, rods?"

Slowly I lifted my eyes to his. "I must wash your dog, Rashidi. That is the law, as it has always been. Then you, Rashidi . . . must do what the law demands of you, as all Americans have done since the beginning of time. Or, at least, since the Eisenhower Administration."

"Me? *Apa?* Rashidi *mesti* what?"

"You must grant me five wishes. Adalai! Stevenson! Hosanna, Adalai Stevenson!"

Oh, the howling. Rashidi, I mean; Buah was much quieter and more pleasant about her very first bath, though I scrubbed and rinsed and brushed until she looked like a Miss Clairol dog. Turned out that parts of her were almost white.

Rashidi was impressed despite himself. And he did honor all three of my wishes—we negotiated. So it certainly wasn't his fault, that in all the miles and miles of jungle rivers we walked in the next two weeks we did not see another *ikan klee* until the day before I left, when we watched two boys pull onto the bank a fish hooked and fought by a bent sapling snare, rather like the kind I've seen used for rabbit, but set with a trigger lashed to fifty-pound-test monofiliment attached to a 5/0 hook baited with a small *ikan* impaled through the tail.

What they showed me wasn't a tenth the size I'd seen running: a fish shaped like a salmon, which looked in the light both gold and silver at once, had the scales of a carp, and a big toothless mouth.

I couldn't even guess what it might be. Ignorance R Us. Twenty years later. . . .

Which leads me back to the tortoise, and one of the very few times a mystery was revealed. . . .

Fast-forward almost a year from my idyll with Rashidi. I am sitting in the staff room of a rural school so far south of Kangar that another twenty miles would put me on the causeway to Singapore.

My mouth is full. My mouth is almost always full, courtesy of the six-foot-tall Chinese woman I am watching intently, whose name could be Siew Kim, but isn't. She's talking as I chew something that explodes against the roof of my mouth. It's a wonderful taste, and it has just occurred to me that Siew has more courage in one hand than survives in most tribes; but neither sensate appreciation nor moral admiration can distract me from the desire to have parts of her body pressed against my tongue. All of her body, at once, if possible.

Naturally I am crazed for her. She may even feel something for me, but her real passion is food, all sorts of which she feeds me, daily, at lunch.

"Admit it," she is saying in excellent, albeit eccentric, English, "Chinese food is the best of all. Fabulous. So much variety. No comparison, I think, to any other cuisine. Please do not debase yourself with objections."

"Debase? Mmm. May I have some more, please? No debasing, I promise."

"That is wise. Because practically anything at all, we can make taste good. Did you know that?"

"Mmm—mm."

Suddenly Siew Kim looks thoughtful. "Even so, I do not think my smaller brother should eat live cock-a-roaches."

"*What?*"

"I do not think so. Not live."

"He eats . . . That is just—"

"Though we Chinese could probably make them taste good. If we wanted."

"What?"

"I am only making a point."

I am at a loss, loath even to swallow whatever is left in my mouth. "Jesus. Jesus, Siew Kim . . . is there *anything*, any animal on *earth* your people won't eat? I mean, anything?"

"Oh yes," she says, cocking her head back with indignation. "Of course. I can tell you one animal that is *much* too sacred to eat."

"You can? What?"

She paused. "You would call it . . . 'tort-us'."

"I would call it . . . wait a minute." I blurt out the story of Tort-us, my Kangar Prize. When I finish, Siew Kim is nodding.

"Yes," she says slowly. "That is the one thing."

"What is?"

"Ah. Well, you see, when a tort-us is out in the world, it is sacred. But if you can catch it," she shrugs.

"Don't tell me. It is a turtle. A God damn turtle."

"Tasting excellent, I can tell you."

* * *

Several months later a desperate-looking Malay Peace Corps employee pounded on my front door. He'd driven all night from Kuala Lumpur, carrying news: that military troops would soon arrive to arrest me for crimes that required no trials to convict, and which carried indeterminate sentences. At the time, the charges seemed so bizarre they might have fallen from the sky; later they appeared inevitable as night.

After hasty packing, and an hour of last-minute moments, as the jungle closed in our headlights while we sped along a highway through . . . after the feeling of disbelief surrendered to alarm, but before I truly understood that I would not see Siew Kim or Rashidi again, nor ever set eyes on an *Ikan Klee*. . . .

I started to laugh. My anxious rescuer, a Malay no doubt terrified at what might happen to him if we were caught, whirled around. "*Apa? Apa?* Why laugh now?"

It was not a question I could answer for him. This was a place where games changed to fit rules, where truth was a shameless slave to agenda. If I was now on my way back through the looking glass, then I only followed the lead of a hapless acquaintance.

That's why I laughed. "Never mind," I said to the driver in Malay. "Never mind." Then, in English, "Poor thing—it's just what the turtle tortoise."

15

The Angler in Winter

The stream has a secret, I am sure. I was told so by somebody who ought to know. It seems like it should—a small water crossed only once by any road. By the time I bushwhack a mile up into the mountain. . . .

How could I not expect snow?

I knew I was in trouble when the eight-mile drive from the nearest town—a reference point I used to locate this stream in my mind—was just shy of vertical, on a road that should have pitons hanging from warning signs reading "Autos Must Carry Carabiners." Soon I find snow in patches. But then, there had been a "dusting" three days earlier—a light fall, I'd read. That might account for the thin white blanket that covers the road, but then it turns into frosting on snowpack probably laid in November. Time for chains, but so close to where I think I should reach the river. . . .

I had made my excuses. "Chasing a story," I said, shifting from foot to foot—but then I always say that. Sophie, almost four years old now, wants to know everything I will see and do, right down to the names of fish I'll catch. Max only smiles. He has little sense of time, so won't miss me. That's what I tell myself.

"You should go," said their mother, which makes me feel peculiar. It means, "Fine, go on," but it's said in a fashion implying I *need* to, had better, that maybe I've been getting a little rough around the edges lately. Which is probably the case: family time is great, the best, except when your mind requires a certain silence, hours or days when you'd better let the pool settle in order to see clearly, consider carefully, make a decision involving your family's future, two careers, your sense of what's possible in the world. Perhaps it's not even the decision that dogs you; it's made, and now all that's left is to accustom yourself to the risk, and to the certainty that only doing something difficult will free you from something dirty. "It's pretty simple," I'd said to her a day or two before, because your family deserves to know why you're taking a risk. "He's stealing from us, and will continue to steal from us, and promises to bankrupt us if we try to reveal what he's doing. And I am going to reveal him. If I can, I'm going to lay him open to the bone."

Blow out the carbon: We liked to pretend this was a real auto-maintenance practice when I was seventeen years old, not an excuse to go fast. I recall the phrase while I'm filling up my aging Honda hatchback, remembering back two decades—almost three?—when we'd kick in a few extra pennies per gallon for high test, fueling for a fishing trip. Then, somewhere down the highway, when the road looked lonely enough, you'd feel the rpm increase, adding beats to the percussion of moving parts, and a new bass line to the chorus of tires hissing on asphalt and the whispered roar of warm air rushing through cracked wing vents.

"Think I'll blow out the carbon," the driver would say, trying not to grin—like a serious guy. Then he'd really put the pedal down, hard and harder, until the acceleration pressing us backward would make us lean forward in defiance, squinting as hair whipped our faces, our open mouths sucking the rush of air. "This should do it!" the driver would shout, as if we'd find this process in the manual: Change oil. Check belts. Go 92 *miles per hour*.

"Right," somebody would shout back with a straight face. Then, inevitably, some fool would crack and start in with that stupid falsetto howling. An idiot would join in, then we'd all be howling and laughing, racing north into mountains toward water, knowing that soon we'd catch a hundred silver trout, battle bass that leaped higher than our heads, and during this one long weekend eat the whole world like a fat apple on a stick.

Unless: "Sorry, officer, just trying to clean out the bores, sir, because you know how Fords are—and exactly what do you do, sir, to run out your cruiser, if you don't mind me asking?"

That Ford: a Galaxie 500. What a car. I could actually see the gas-gauge needle drop at any speed over seventy, even though it was measuring a tank that held most of a middle-sized dinosaur, I imagined, or maybe three, depending on how those things melted down into crude oil. A boat, that car was, solid and strong—never let you down. It had been my father's, so smelled of pipe smoke, one aromatic blend or another. I guess that only compounded my assumption that nothing could go too awfully wrong on any voyage. Nothing that couldn't be made right.

And of course, I could sleep stretched out in the back seat, and did, beside waters in Arizona, California, New Mexico, and Colorado. I had done so, a night between two days of playing with bluegills in lower Lake Pleasant, outside Phoenix, circa 1972, near a spot where I could wade a small bay, throwing hideous Korean "hand-tieds" toward shore. A fellow was watching from the shade beneath a palo verde tree: a prison guard from Yuma, he turned out to be. Like me, he was a self-taught devotee, each of us "the only fly fisherman I know." He'd discovered what he thought was an astonishing fishery for black bass in oxbows and sloughs off the Colorado River. "I mean, I don't even know what I'm doing, and I catch two-pounders all the time, ten or a dozen in a couple of hours. And I have it all to myself, always, so call me if you ever come that way."

For a long time I hoped to, some day. I imagined him stalking shallows the way he described, alone on a finger of flat water, banks of reeds defining his horizon. He'd be working a whippy fiberglass 7-weight, I knew, from barely light through dawn and an hour or two past that. Never later: in Yuma, they don't just fry eggs on the sidewalk, they sear steaks, and toss turkeys into the shade to roast slowly.

I had mentioned those cooking facts to my fellow solo artist, the prison guard. He said he hated the heat, but liked his job okay, might move when he had seniority. He seemed resolved to me, not resigned. "It's good for my family right now, so I figure I'll stay." And he did have the river with all these bass. "Remember, you give me a call."

I hoped to—and might have, several years later and so many years ago now, recollecting the invitation late in a spring night when I smelled water five miles east of the Colorado River, approaching from the Arizona side. But I did remember his name, and could call the next morning from a pay phone at the border-crossing station. That left me the night.

I drove across the bridge, took the first exit, then cut back on a sandy track toward a choir of frogs, a million at least, peepers each suggesting "popper" to me. In a littered pull-off at the water's edge, I parked and, stripped down to my cutoffs, leaned on the Galaxie's hood to survey a stretch of river. The night was moonless, but by the ambient light of stars and cars I could make out currents muscling each other, moving countless tons. The Colorado is a heavy river, this far down, muddy and massy and slovenly, a little. Two or three times a minute I'd see a swirl or tiny vortex, which I tried to imagine were fish, but the flotsam was real enough. I saw a broken branch, mats of reeds, then the billowing sail of a plastic bag sweeping toward black shadows behind a bridge abutment. The air was just about the temperature of breath, smelling faintly of fresh clams and weeds, wet enough to soften the rimes of salt sweat left on my skin by the drive through the desert.

I waited for nothing in particular, save perhaps to let my body let go of the road trembles. For a moment, I thought I could hear water whispering through the tules, a braided sound, like a woman brushing her hair. The urgent frogs quickly obscured this, so loud together they almost drowned the fall-away roars of trucks on the highway.

The water's too high, I suddenly suspected. If that was true, it was too bad . . . but only that. The Colorado was not my destination, because I didn't have one.

"From here, I can go anywhere I want to," I thought. "Anywhere at all. Anywhere I can write and fish." Sure. I'd spend a week or three in Leucadia, stalking corbina in the breakers of a rising tide, staying low to see them limned in the waves of an early sun that rose behind my left shoulder. And on the same beach, late at night, bonfires would flicker at my back, around which party people would drink and sing while I wrestled enough leopard sharks to fill my mother's freezer. Dense, meaty fillets: shark's the only fish that almost answered my father's lament, the same as anybody's who diets for his heart, "Where's the beef?"

After that? Perhaps back to the bar I'd tended outside Denver, at a country club where in the evenings I worked tiny keel streamers through a water hazard, for big crappies and small walleyes, once a three-pound largemouth. Or to L.A., maybe, where a favorite professor had engineered an introduction to a graduate school I knew nothing about. I could write scripts and fish for bonito at the Redondo Beach outflow. Or up to San Francisco, as a new literary agent suggested, where I might hunt striped bass while making a novel from a short story in which a broken boy had a perfect day, fishing for pike in a prairie reservoir outside Kiowa, Colorado.

"Anywhere I want," I said silently to the frogs, feeling loose in the limbs, liquid. At my feet, water I might have fished in the Rockies moved Grand Canyon silt south. Yet even a river that carves a continent is compelled, headed in a direction determined eons ago. *But I can go anywhere I want, do anything I'm able.*

I thrilled to think that, then, quiet, listened again. And grinned, remembering why it was the frogs sang. Adding—at their suggestion you might say—"With anyone who'll come along for the ride."

The back seat of the Galaxie had just enough give. Real Naugahyde trimming, you bet, along the edges of a dark red fabric, some smooth synthetic, which, incredibly, still remembered the complicated scents of a girl I probably had loved before I knew how to know that.

The flow was too high, I saw at dawn. Unfishable, unless perhaps you knew the sloughs. Driving back to the pay phone at the border-crossing station, I was amazed at how green the land looked all along the river. Yuma in bloom. How about that.

My prison guard's name wasn't in the book.

Of course not. A prison guard meets unpleasant people, the kind you wouldn't want having anything to do with you and yours. Predators—or worse, people who prefer to do damage, kill for sport, lie when the truth would do, just for the pleasure of lying. . . .

Too much, lately, I've had to deal with people like that.

So ends the reverie, but it carries me almost to Winters before my mind snaps back to meaner exigencies, into a morning nearly dark as that night on the Colorado River, and much harder edged. The barometer is falling, I can tell, and cold air leaking around the window tightens skin around my eyes. Twenty-five years ago, I headed west from the Arizona border, then north—so now I am here. In the interim I have done things I wanted. Today I am as bound as any river by responsibilities, by gravity.

Beneath a close, gray sky, not far from a church long deserted, I meet snow drifts just too deep. I know, because I test them.

"Can't be," I think. I have to get through. Because in my life now there is little time, and I cannot come back here, this year, gambling that a surprise might make a story.

The quiet is thick. The kind that makes you feel there might be sounds just beyond hearing.

Wait.

It's not actually the stream I hear, but water trickling down a hill beside the road, snowmelt making tiny crackling noises as it flows beneath a crust of crummy ice. I sink through this to the top of my shoe, but not before I'm certain the slope leads to my destination.

Gear up. Sweater, vest, jacket. I pull the hood over my hat. Neoprene waders and some studded boots new to me. Also new: a staff I've wanted to test. I hesitate over that, then secure it to my lanyard.

Really lousy snow, but the footing beneath it is good. I'm not a hundred feet into the woods when I see the stream.

High water—much higher than I expected. Clear, or that peculiar tint streams seem to have when very cold, perhaps just the reflection of dark sky. Though it's barely afternoon, the world lacks color—has, really, only grays and dark greens edged with browns nearly black. The stream I can see splits around a three-boulder island.

I watch for a minute, waiting not for rises, which I know I won't see, but for—what? A sound, perhaps. Some signal. An omen.

None comes, so I start to hum, and make my way down.

In a shallow channel I rake a few rocks to screen the stream. There's practically nothing in the mesh. I hate it when that happens. I sample again. Two specks move: when they're that size it takes a jeweler's loupe to tell mayfly nymphs from just-hatched stones. I test the water temperature after rinsing the babies back in. Feels like low forties for both the seconds it takes to numb my fingers.

You never know. At least I'm certain the fish ain't overheated and overfed. Attractor time: a Green Wulff trailing a Brassie from the bend, that's the ticket, a combo I like to think of as a big burger on top and a small fry below—and you'll eat the tidbit if the main meal looks suspicious. So rigged, I wade around the boulder island to work the far channel, edging toward a slow run below a riffle. Seriously good-looking little hole there.

Nothing doing.

After working another pool with my Wulff and Brassie, I switch to the Brassie alone, to get the fly deep. Five or six casts later the leader twitches. I strike backhand and miss. I'll try again, but I don't much like my position, standing on the shoulder of a giant boulder, casting upstream around a corner. It looks like if I can get around, though, or go up and over, I'll have a better shot from the other side.

As I begin to move my attention is on the cast I'll make, the slack I'll throw to the drift. Though I am high up, the footing is good. I see that the top of the boulder tilts down toward a large crease in the rock where a patch of snow has drifted and packed. I test the edge and find it firm. If I step far enough out to the center, the next step will put me across, back on stone, so I only swing out the staff to steady me, just in case, and it pierces through the snow crust like a hot needle, stabbing through what might as well be nothing and will support nothing, material so loose beneath the smooth surface that the staff continues to fall right through to the handle as I let it go and drop backward onto the tilted top of the rock, striking hard even as my studded heels rake for traction, mauling the stone as they propel me away from a peril vivid even in dreams—*falling*—until I lie still, knowing myself safe, finally, with butt and back pressing the boulder hard enough that I can, suddenly, breathe.

One hand steadies me. But it is toward the other that I cast a desperate eye—the one clenched at the end of a stiff arm that is still thrusting my rod skyward in what looks now like a wild gesture of triumph, but was actually just an earnest appeal—"Take it Lord! it's a Wojneki four-weight and I'm falling fast . . . !"

"Oh, my."

Those aren't exactly the words I use, but they convey some of my feeling. I am a little damaged—bruised, but with rod intact. I know these things before I actually become clear on the concept. What happened? After a minute spent staring at the sky, I am convinced of only two things: it will snow pretty soon, and I will live to see it.

It wasn't a crease in the boulder I was trying to cross, but a cleft between two boulders, cracked apart from each other sometime in the past. It wasn't a patch of snow on which I leaned my staff, but a rotten bridge. From below I reach up with my rod to determine how far I would have fallen. Less than a mile—say, ten feet from my boot soles, which means my head would travel almost sixteen. If the old noggin tapped granite on the way down? If one leg snapped, or two?

Bad. Bad enough that I inhale deeply.

But that's about all.

I mean, it's not like something similar to this hasn't happened before, during one close call or another in life, ninety percent of which have occurred while driving. Sure, it's sobering. A reminder. The problem right now, however, is that it will start snowing soon.

I head back downstream. By the time I near the place where I first reached the creek I am composed, even a little lighthearted. I know that, the way these stories go, I should experience an epiphany, a moment of revelation. And I have before. Just not this time, though I would appreciate a little glass of something brown.

"Pretty soon," I think, as I pause to look down at that little three-boulder island.

Wham. Just like that—not one epiphany, but *two*. At once. Well, maybe one epiphany and one revelation, but who's counting.

The first one is huge, an obvious cliché with a kicker. If it had words: "The world is a place where you can fall hard and die." And if I had fallen, these things would be true: the cold would find me before anybody, and my family would be cheated of what they deserve because I was not alive to fight a battle I must—there's no choice. Oh my.

Then, right on top of these dire and important realizations, comes this: *"Dunce!* That channel you screened for bugs an hour ago is dry all summer—of course nothing lives there. The question is, what's alive in the main streambed?"

The thing about epiphanies is that once you've had one, you're not likely to lose it soon. They keep. So if you've got something profound to think about, but only half an hour to fish . . . muse later.

I seine the main stem. Green rock worms—there they are, three of them about size 14, a fourth that's almost a 12. There's a cranefly larva, one of the dirty-cream-colored ones with that faintly iridescent—what? Membrane?

Second cast.

The fish is big, sluggish and slow, a brown better than I had imagined catching. Not a lunker, by any means, but a trout to smile about.

I have an odd moment, as I cradle it. I want to believe this was just a thought or two distorted by the fall, or by the shock of having had two epiphanies—1.5, anyway—at once. Maybe, but instead of the usual appreciative rumble that fish prompt from me, I think instead: *You would have killed what you thought this fly was because that's what you are and what you do. And I could kill you right now with nothing more than a squeeze for no more reason than because I want to. That's the way it is. I would kill you, if I needed to. I won't because I don't, and that's who I am.*

"Goodbye," I said.

By the time I reach the highway, it's snowing. Big, luminous flakes. It's not a whiteout, only heavy going, and it's thirty miles to where I intend to sleep.

Suddenly, I laugh, although not out loud.

Well, shoot.

I find a pull-off that I know will be plowed, if worst comes to worst, and that has trees along two sides.

I lay one of the back seats flat, roll out a mat, a blanket, then an old sleeping bag onto which I pile two sweaters and my jacket.

Snug, it is.

I lie quiet, almost still. Tomorrow, I will find fishable water somewhere down the mountain—

No. No, I won't.

Tomorrow I will go home, I realize slowly. Home is the only place I should go from here, there to do something I must. That's my life now; no regrets.

I relax slowly, let the warm weights of wool and surety rest on my chest. I am not resigned, but resolute, at ease enough that at last I begin to smile, listening to the snow falling heavy in the trees.

The sound reminds me of a river, moving through reeds.

Then, of a woman, brushing her hair.

16

Missionary Positions for Tree Huggers and Stream Stewards

About a year ago I met somebody on the phone—nice fellow—who said with a "be reasonable" tone, "But that Ted Williams, you will admit, is way over the top."

The characterization made me cringe. This Ted Williams writes conservation columns for *Audubon Magazine* and *Fly Rod & Reel*, and his work often appears in *Trout*, the *Atlantic Salmon Journal*, and *Living Bird*. "If you believe that about him," I answered unhappily, "it's because the rest of us have gotten so lazy and dull and indulgent that we're just not doing our jobs."

Too true. As it happens, it's also true that one good reason I started aiming writing in the niche of angling was to avoid the entanglements of dirty journalism, having retreated from muckraking adventure to trout waters and the "culture" of fly fishing. Can *you* think of better shelter?

Even so, I could not altogether avoid issues. How can any of us? If your eyes are open and you see your favorite stream full of suds, literally foaming at the mouth, you do what? Laundry? Should our home-town team have said of the poisoned Sacramento River, "Finally that damn streambed's clean; now let's keep it that way"? The prospects of the Trinity River may depend on the letters of support sent in by concerned fly fishers. So?

On the other hand . . .

I don't want to know. I don't. Life is full of dire news and we're all dying, thanks very much. Fly fishing is my pleasure and passion: when I pick up a magazine dedicated to this subject I'm not hoping for a read about water wars. Not at all—"Writer, let us have wine! Bring me women and trout! Children to tickle and toss in the air! More women! Bigger trout! Good Editor, give me Shakespeare in the park where there's a stream with a great brown under every bank and riffles exploding with rainbows made hysterical by hatching caddis! I want articles about bonefish in my backyard cruising through the morning dew, dorado gangs roaming the freeways, feeding on Crips! Forget stats on agribiz—sing me epics of brave fishers in small boats hauled into the sunset by stripers—and hauled back the next morning! Show me how to tie scuds—then give me recipes for cooking the real critters in curry! Draw diagrams for dances we may do wading wet—tangos and tarantellas! Send me cognac with my next subscription! And how about cartoons? Sheridan Anderson style, only with Piscator Dinosaur and Nancy Nympher—stuff I can use to tempt my sons and daughters, inspiring them to cry, 'Up, up, Old Daddy of ours! We pray you to take us fishing at that favorite place of yours, that fine stream you fished as a child, about which you tell wonderful stories, and call—' "

Love Canal.

Reality: what a bitch. "The bastards won't let you live," howled Gerald Green, in the *The Last Angry Man*, meaning to my mind that if we don't fight for our waters we lose them. We've already lost a lot of them and here's a secret: *you know that*. You might even be a Marty Seldon or Richard Iszmerian or Jim Edmundson or Bob Baiocchi or Byron Lydecker or somebody else who's been fighting the good fight for two or five decades.

Or, you might be more like me, in which case you're probably wondering, "When will the man get back to the sex and trout part?"

Another secret: editors know (most) readers don't want to read (much) about conservation. Fishing isn't first a "cause" to you; so it's wiser to run a how-to or where-to than "Heavy Metals Infiltrate Everywhere" and "Great Lakes Evaporate" and "Corporate Farmers Reveal 'God Says The Trinity's Water Is for Us, Really, We All Heard Him.' " For most readers, myself included, the effect of opening a fishing magazine to find stories of environmental disasters is, shall we say, dampening? Resembling rather how newlyweds might feel if their wedding night was co-opted by an in-law proctologist showing slides. . . .

But what's more important? A few hours of excitement? Or Hygiene Hints That May Save Your Life?

And yet, the question remains: Is there a way to combine what it is we want to learn with what we ought to know? To balance our pursuit of pleasure with the efforts we must make to preserve the world where our pleasure may be found?

Probably not. But I suggest that we at least contemplate ourselves as readers with brutal objectivity, as Machiavelli might have done. Omit for the moment the folks who are especially fine and good and dutiful about this. What would get the rest of us to do what we should?

Begin with what works today in other markets: "Sex sells," say the ad guys; but it's a hard angle for us to exploit. Too bad, but we can only dream about the possibilities: "Barbless and Topless," "Support Wild Trout for Wilder Parties," "United Anglers' Ms. Catch-and-Release Admits 'I Always Whip-Finish My Man.'"

C'est la vie. So what else?

"Dire threat" is the angle most often worked in environmental articles. And worked. And worked again. For good reason, too: the public sentiment that allowed passage of the Clean Water Act—arguably the most important measure to remedy environmental damages in this country—swelled from reactions to *Time* magazine's blazing images of the Lower Cuyahoga River. I'd almost forgotten this famous Great Lakes tributary; I met it again while writing an *Outdoor Life* piece on rivers that have come back from disaster. What surprised me was that *Time*'s scorching imagery was mainly hyperbole: although this stretch of the Cuyahoga was indeed ruined, nearly lifeless, one may doubt that "the river oozes rather than flows," or wonder if in its depths "a person does not drown, but decays." In point of fact, what people believed was polluted water burning in a conflagration that lasted for days was actually an ignited oil spill extinguished in twenty minutes.

But dire worked then, and has since—many times; and rarely does it need to rely on exaggeration. Things really are as bad as Ted Williams says. The problem, however, is that competition is so intense in the fields of fear, with news of inadequate flows for summer-run steelhead competing with reports of Rwandan genocide, Hurricane Edgar, the latest flesh-eating virus or boxer. Most of us are dired out most of the time; those sounding the alarms must clamor more loudly and more urgently until the noise makes people want to give up and go fishing.

So, no sex, and now dire is deadening our nerves . . . what else?

I was reminded of an often neglected approach—what we might call "the Brightwater Gambit"—while standing in front of the whirling-disease booth at a recent trade show.

"Nobody wants to talk to me," said the glum guy manning the display. "I raise the specter of death, and nobody wants to know."

Neither did I. But a month before I'd ended an all-night drive from Montana to fish Martis Lake, where I intended to wade the spit and turn a few trout heads. I reached for my boots and noticed they were still damp. Going to be cold, I thought, then shook my head, remembering the Madison. . . .

Wait a minute.

Needless to say, I fished in other shoes. And the question generated that day was the one I'd approached the booth to have answered: "What's the bleach-to-water ratio I should use to sterilize waders?"

"You know, I'm not sure. Some amount of bleach."

I could just see "some amount" melting holes in neoprene.

Then it struck me. "Tell you what," I said, choosing the words carefully. "I'll bet you that most of the folks in this room would like to know that recipe. I bet it could get you free press all over, and lots of attention, because cleaning waders is something people can do, and probably would if they knew how. And you know how it goes once people start doing the right thing . . . you catch my drift?"

"I think I do," he said. "That might work."

I think so too, but I never heard from him.

There's another tactical move we can make that might attend this one, one that acknowledges a similar challenge we face: it's difficult to properly credit people for what they've done. Especially when they don't act in hope of gaining recognition—which is yet another way in which fly fishers may differ from oil companies, politicians, and narcissists. As it stands, ninety percent of the literate public can name a hoopster thug who choked his coach, but practically nobody has heard of a guy whose insight inspired the rescue of one of the country's prettiest rivers, the Cranberry, in West Virginia, and who helped develop a technology that may save hundreds or thousands of other streams. I mean, which man and story deserves endless attention? Never mind for a moment the ludicrous question: "So who should get millions of dollars for their achievement?"

My answer to this anonymity? "Knights of Brightwater," I propose. We're talking playing cards and a TV series with quick cuts and jerky camera movements and, for younger viewers, Discovery Channel–style close-ups of rejuvenated insect populations grazing healthy greenery when smelts attack—then big fish gobbling the smaller, that sort of thing. All this while the narrative rumbles "If not for Sir Bob, Keeper of Ransome Creek, this lush landscape would be as empty of life as your toilet, bleak as study hall. . . ."

In other words, a cultural revolution. *"I dub thee Sir Williams. . . ."*

And in the meantime, perhaps we should merely pretend that every article written by somebody other than Ted Williams contains a secret preface which reads "If Somebody Takes Care." *If somebody takes care,* "You'll do well fishing a midge slow and deep." *Thanks to the following people and organizations*, "This stream holds some fine brookies, and sometimes Dolly Varden." Perhaps you might even imagine a phrase beneath the masthead of your favorite magazine—This Publication Made Possible by People Who Battle for the Waters Where Fish Live.

And if by chance you are one of those people . . .

Smile, Sir or Lady, and imagine yourself a byline.

17

———

Here's To You

———

"**Y**ou see, Mr. Locke, we hoped that since you're both an angler and an investigator, you might understand what others would not." Harris hesitated, then leaned his bulk forward and gazed at me intently. There was faith in his face, and great expectation. I thought he looked disturbingly like a Labrador retriever expecting a duck.

"I see," I said. Then I waited, which did not have the desired effect; so, finally, "You presumed I would understand . . . what?"

"That fly fishermen do not murder people. They simply don't."

Silly generalization, of course, though I couldn't recall any fly-fishing killers offhand. Claus Von Bulow? For a moment I contemplated this new and unique line of criminal defenses: "Armed robbery, Your Honor? Impossible: my client fishes dry flies. Move to dismiss." When I emerged from this exercise, however, it was to read Harris's stare. He would buy that, I realized. As a juror, that would be all the evidence he needed.

Then it happened. Some men fall to elegant lines of leg, to stud games, or to junk bonds at 200 percent a year. So would I if given the chance, but instead I'm reamed by affection for the honest fool, an honorable naïf, some Don Quixote eager to tilt at a Trans Am full of gang-bangers with Uzis.

People like Harris.

"Excuse me," I said gently. "This is Oakland, California. A rather tough town, as you may have heard. In Oakland, Mr. Harris . . . dead people don't kill people. And that's only a general rule."

"Even so," he replied.

"Even so what?" I snapped.

Harris actually smiled, pleased that we now shared this secret.

—From *Dead Drift*, a detective novel moldering in my file cabinet.

After writing this purely fictional scene I read it to Steve Gore, a friend and private investigator with whom I've fished and worked for decades. In one capacity or another, Steve has interviewed thousands of criminals in the last twenty-five years. "The question is," I said, "have you ever met a crook who fly fished?"

Steve considered. "Once had a burglar who bait fished for steelhead."

"Well, sure. But a fly fisher?"

"Not so far."

How about *that*.

Several times now I've tried to approach a topic that would, stripped of veils, read something like "On the Honor of Fly Fishers." But writing a paean to decency is dicey—and what's the point? Especially when fly fishers on the whole want little to do with descriptions of themselves en masse and tremble at any notion of elitism.

There is a point. Several. The newest one is named Max, a son of mine now seven months old, who so far seems to be the happiest person I've ever met. And why not? He can flirt his way across entire grocery stores—the warehouse kind, no less—leaving men grinning and women weak in the knees. It's something to see, awesome; I call him the "Puppy Buddha" and regularly ask Lisa who his father is, *really*.

Because of daughter Sophie, and now Max, I must scour the world for redeeming features. I do this every morning, right after reading the paper, or immediately following those fits of gagging the news produces.

It ain't easy. But I'm trying.

Have tried: "No ordinary fly fisher exists," I wrote in an abandoned essay. "And now that I've bowed to the good god of right thinking, I should very much like to describe Everyman with the Long Rod."

Everywoman also—see the Dame. By "ordinary" I mean the kind of dedicated practitioner whom marketing demographers try to describe, and who can only be sketched with smoke in the breeze: educated or maybe not, but thinks and reads; quieter than most, usually, but attentive; cautious by nature though not timid; unusually generous, honest, and committed to a sense of fair play.

"Right," says the cynic. "You wish."

And how long has Cynic been suffering these spells? Because they can be surgically corrected.

It happens that I know of eight or ten crooks in fly fishing, all of them "in the business," about evenly spread through manufacturing, sales, publishing, guiding, and trading in endangered animal parts. One has a felony record that I'm aware of, another stands accused and so will a third soon, with luck. They're predators, attracted to the sport primarily by a pool of marks with money. The ones I've met share an attitude: "These rich fools will believe anything and so deserve to be robbed by a great man like me." (Narcissism, I'm convinced, has more to do with crime than nastiness, and vastly more than need.) They see an industry in which, until recently, many people expected to rely on handshakes; they recognize each of these folks as meat on a stick. They believe that small companies that can't afford to patent products, or defend the patents they have, deserve ugly fates. They are among us, these crooks.

When you consider fly fishers, however—the sportsmen and women themselves—think on this: a fly shop owner I know insists that in fourteen years of doing business he has had a total of two bounced checks. *Two*, out of thousands.

Why is that?

I'll return to that question. I mean, as if I knew.

One day my friend Bob Small and I were just hanging around looking cool when out of the blue I asked him a question I'd been pondering for a while. Bob, I should note, took up fly fishing right after retirement, without having angled much before that, so the gist of my query was this: What aspect of the sport drew him in?

He answered in a flash. "Generosity. The generosity of fly fishers I met."

An unexpected reply, yet I wasn't surprised. I knew Bob had been befriended by a New Zealand local while wandering South Island—a Kiwi who took Bob out on a lake one moonless night, hooked up a three-pound rainbow, then handed Bob the rod—"The thrill of my life."

Unusual, this hosting? Naw. I've had any number of incidents in which fly fishers, encountered on a stream or elsewhere, have gone well out of their way to help. Usually it's to offer a fly or bit of advice, but I've had strangers politely ask if they might show me a whole rigging system they thought appropriate—like the first time I visited

Pyramid Lake, where a pair of anglers tied me a Maxima leader with (one each) of their Crystal Buggers, then insisted I keep a handful more flies in case the fish ever came in.

Kind? Yes. An earth-shaking event? No, unless you happen to think, as I often do, that courtesy and decency have more to do with civilization than Congress understands. Unique to fly fishing? Surely not, though in the decade I played golf, nobody tossed me a new ball, saying "Try this one; the dimples have done wonders for me." Are there obnoxious exceptions to what seems like a generous rule? Boy, are there. One of the worst I've heard about came from the radio producer for whom I work, who was visiting the Abaco Island chain on her honeymoon when her hubby discovered he'd forgotten his fly boxes. Disaster . . . but no! There on the ferry was another fly fisher, an American, geared to the teeth. *Not one fly would this fisher lend him*, not even a hook to tie on.

Incredible. Even so, if I had an hour to spend with every angler I've heard make a generous offer to draw a map, tie a knot, demonstrate technique or critique a backcast; if I could have visited half of those who've offered their homes and time to host classes in tying or rod building; if I'd just drunk coffee or bourbon with every one who seemed eager to share a smile and a story. . . .

Man, what an angler I'd be today. Caffeine-toxic, maybe, and surely an alcoholic, but well informed by the kindness of strangers who I suspect make awfully good friends.

The kind of friends Max will need.

And among them, I hope, he will also find a niche in the larger social order. Or find at least a sense that, somewhere, obscured by the unfolding entropy of American Culture, there are strangers he can trust, mostly.

Your kids might need the same, if you have them. Maybe you need that sense, too.

Maybe not, but it was partly the influence of such trust that lead me to the community of fly fishers, on a journey I recalled last year while writing a speech for the Granite Bay Fly Fishers. The board of that club elected to hold open for me a speaking engagement, when complications with Max's incubation made any scheduling dicey. Max appeared on time, so I did too, making these observations.

Private Investigator Gore and I met shortly after I settled in the Bay Area, the mid-1970s. For fifteen years we fished this state hard, from the Kern River north to the Klamath, from the coast to Truckee and a lot of places in between. Over time and through bitter experience we developed a set of rules for stashing gear. Here's a sampling:

While fishing at night off piers in Oakland and Berkeley, leave your car doors open, since the vermin are going to get in one way or another and you might as well save the window glass. (Burglarized in Berkeley; lost a fly rod.)

On warmwater lakes, hide everything, lock up, and pray. (Burglarized at Lake Berryessa; lost a fly rod. Also saw slews of burglarized vehicles on the Feather River: I suspect stealing from anglers is one of the Oroville area's larger industries, ranking somewhere after welfare fraud and methamphetamine production.)

When parked near most mountain trout streams, locking the door is enough.

And on fly-fishing-only waters, *feel free to leave the doors open and your wallet on the dashboard.*

The "McCloud River Protocol," I came to call this system, eventually, named for the honorable end of it. I wouldn't test it too often—yeah, I'm sure somebody's been ripped off at Ah-di-na—but I bet it would often pass.

When Steve stopped fishing I meandered solo for years. I stuck to our rules, gravitating mostly toward mountain waters, where I sought out and met those surprisingly helpful fly fishers. I'd written pieces for *Field &*

Stream and *Gray's Sporting Journal;* I changed aim. And when Steve and I did an exposé of police corruption, it was to trout waters I fled for a time.

To this day, I ponder reasons that might explain this McCloud River protocol, along other generalizations I've made here. I've groped, been baffled by the enormous variety of fly fishers. But still . . . there's something here, something to this. I wrestled the ideas again when Sophie was born. Now I'm assembling for her and Max, for my older kids—for me—an explanation. Something formal. It will take a while, but I read this draft to Max the other day, when his diaper was fresh and his mind keenly focussed:

"Listen, Max, and never mind the big words:

> Fly fishing is a fundamentally predatory behavior styl-
> ized by tradition—a blood sport full of art and science,
> bound by ethical strictures. Fly fishers pledge to honor
> suspiciously chivalrous codes in order to catch crea-
> tures completely wild, alien, and indifferent to delicate
> rules. That paradox—this elaborate approach to a
> primitive activity—seems to have special appeal to
> moralists of many sorts, from eco-conservatives to
> unabashed liberals, anarchists and other dreamers.
> Their gratification derives, I believe, from a sense that
> in this one realm of life there is a natural order, a place
> for integrity, and for fair play.

"How's that? Huh? So now you know, boy-o of mine, why it is that you're named

> Max
> McCloud
> Norman."
> (Old Max just smiled.)

18

McCumber and Sons

I fished McCumber Reservoir on the cusp—early in summer, before algae scummed its surface. A mountain impoundment, steep-sided along most of its bank, McCumber is ringed around with trees and in places impaled by dead trunks of pine.

Good float-tubing water, for a fly fisher. I launched at a corner of the dam, intending to fin away and find solitude, but the rainbows had schooled there. So had the fishermen; so I shared several acres with a pram, another tuber, and a boat tied off to the buoy line fifty feet out from the concrete spillway.

All by itself the boat crew made an oppressive crowd. Five men sat in the fourteen-foot Sears aluminum job, and I'd bet a fly box that three of them had felony records; that's an educated guess, since I spent two years conducting in-jail interviews. From two hundred feet away I could hear all their conversation, if conversation is what you call a collection of obscenities used as verbs, nouns, commas and periods, and as all-f—king-purpose sounds to fill in life's little f—king gaps, if you know what I mean.

The fish were there, no question. I took and released one, the pram fellow cleverly scored three, and the boat party steadily filled an ice chest with trout bewildered by green pheromone paste. From the beginning I'd been tired of hearing them. Pretty soon one was causing me to grind enamel off my molars.

The loudest had a son of seven or eight standing on the spillway, a boy who had already adopted the aggressive whine of the maltreated. Every few minutes he begged to join his elders in the overcrowded craft. "You said, Dad. You *said*."

"Did I? Well f—k me then," Dad would answer, or variations on this theme. "You can f—kin' swim out here, if you f—king want to."

"But you *said*, Dad."

"Yeah? So what? Why don't you shut the f—k up? Or do you want your f—kin' ass kicked?"

Dad's wit was clearly designed as much to please his cronies as to provide moral instruction to his offspring. A chorus of low laughter often suggested he succeeded on the first front.

Enough already. A dozen fish was hardly worth such entertainment. Better to practice casting in dead water. I pedal-paddled away toward the lake's far end, where shallow water was glazed by mid-morning sun.

A hundred yards out I could still glory in the boaters' casual profanity. It infected me—and others, I realized, as I passed a quiet boat where fished two old men and a boy. The four of us stared silently from beneath the beaks of our hats. Nobody nodded. Nobody waved.

Another hundred yards and I still wanted away, but a swirl near the bank surprised me. Certainly the water was too shallow there, too warm, to encourage a trout to hunt this time of day?

The next swirl was so violent that a shower of shiners burst through the surface, scattering outward from a boil like tossed autumn leaves. I felt some panic myself while knotting on a streamer.

My first cast didn't make the distance. The second did and the fly never sank—slash, like *that*. Good fish, too, a brown trout longer than a foot—and isn't it strange, to find him in so close?

Yes, but he wasn't the exception: before I'd slipped the hook another fish broke the surface, right on shore again, not thirty feet away. Way too shallow, way too warm. . . .

He hit and missed, hit, missed, refused me. Then a third fish performed a "come hither" half a hundred feet down. I followed, took him, felt my fins churn in weeds three feet below me.

More fish came up. I simply couldn't believe their daring—had they no respect for ospreys? Certainly the water was off color, but how long would they hazard these adventures, this near to noon?

Long enough that I found them all the way to the inlet, a delta where I was practically wading flats, casting to raiders that nosed reeds apart in water no deeper than my knees. Two throws took fish that churned weeds into salad-sized pieces. Browns come up, of course, when they can't burrow down, and so these twisted on top, chopping with their heads.

By one o'clock the action had faded, so I finned back to the dam in bright sunlight. On the way I acknowledged myself lots more lucky than smart. I would not have guessed to find fish under the conditions encountered; I'd persevered only because the risers insisted. Fish and learn. The wisest among us is only playing the odds.

I did another kind of calculation when I saw the Sears boat still tethered to the buoy line. At the rate I'd seen them killing, their limits must be long exhausted—and how long had they been there when I launched?

It didn't relieve me when they fell silent on my approach. Then, from a new character on the spillway, "Say, Roddy, how many you got now?"

There was a snicker in the voice, a joke implicit. "None," f—k-dad shouted back. "Haven't got a one yet." Laughter followed.

I kicked toward the corner where dam met bedrock, easing my way past a weed bed. In the shadows beneath a tree I saw a figure holding a rod—the boy I'd seen earlier in the boat. I would need to cross his line to beach.

"Excuse me," I called to him softly.

"Sure," he answered, and reeled in.

I confess that I am spoiled for kids. My stepchildren have done this to me. A decade ago they said, "We adopt you," and though their mother and I split three years later, the kids' commitment, and mine, has never even come into question. With every reason to turn delinquent, that trio fills rooms with plaques and trophies and sweaters with letters; they fill the air with laughter and fill my arms each time we say hello and goodbye. I don't get it, I take no credit; but I am spoiled to the bone. Certainly I don't mind a boy with a Mohawk haircut and earring—hell, Marc once shaved into his head the emblem of a favorite running shoe—or a girl with white lipstick and black fingernails. But I don't like what my own call "attitude."

This boy had none. Yellow-haired, twelve years old or thirteen, he stepped back for me, eyes attending my float tube and my rod. "You were fly fishing, weren't you," he said softly.

"Yes."

"Is it hard to learn to do that?"

"A little," I admitted. "But it's worth it."

He nodded appraisingly. "I bet it is," he said firmly.

That made me smile again. But when I saw f—k-dad's children in the parking lot, my mood turned foul. I was a dirty child, for certain, forever grubbing earth and water for snakes and tadpoles. But these kids were filthy in a very different way.

They left an hour later, weeping as their father f—k-bullied them into his van. Two pick-ups hauled off their felon company and God knows how many fish. The few settlers left in the campground seemed to sigh with collective relief.

Across lunch dishes at my camper's little table, I saw again the yellow-haired boy. He'd found an open slot between pines, and now patiently flogged the dirt with a fly rod.

I thought about it, took my time—I was still soggy and tired—but who could resist the echo of "I bet it is"? Or, for that matter, the boy's response to the offer of help: "Yes, sir. I'd really appreciate that." In ten minutes he made it clear that a more earnest student would be hard to find.

Five minutes after that one of the older men from the boat rushed out from the campsite adjacent—big old fellow, charging like a bison.

I stepped back. It's a hard world we live in these days, and a parent or grandparent's protection is too often needed. I understand that.

"Excuse me, mister," he grumbled, "but it's been thirty years since I handled that rod, and I was never any good. Wonder if I can take a lesson with the boy?"

Half an hour later we left the kid to his homework. The old fellow wanted to share some secrets of the lake he'd fished for twenty years. From the dam he traced the drowned river's old and surprising path—to the east, not the middle of the lake—and recalled days when a five-pound brown was not exceptional. His information was valuable and valued; we talked on, eventually arriving at the subject of f—k-dad and his son. At that topic the old man's voice dropped to a whisper. He even hunched a little as he spoke. "Could you believe it, the way he was talking, in front of his son? And the way he talked *to* him. . . . Terrible. Terrible."

We sighed together. By way of shaking off these thoughts I said, "Well, I'm sure it's a pleasure for you, having a grandson so well mannered. He must make good company in your boat."

I'd thought to compliment, but the old fellow looked stricken. "Oh, yes, he is," he murmured. "Good company, I mean. He's not mine, though. Grandson of my pal." When he looked out across the lake his sadness was open and profound. "No, not mine. My grandkids—hell, I hate to say it, but when my son said he wanted them to stay with me up here, I told him that I was coming back to town. I wasn't, you see, not for a week; now I have to. Those children don't behave for my wife and me any better than they do for their folks, and I knew we couldn't take seven days of them. Hell of a thing."

Yes, it is.

I thought too much about the man's regret in the next several days. I still do. It struck me hard when I telephoned home to my answering machine and heard a message from Marc, my oldest: "Just wanted to find out if you're back yet, how your trip went, make sure you're okay." I choked a little at that, and laughed. Because it's my nature I tried to think out how such a relationship evolved, and why a kindly old man must return a week early from fishing. Something in the McCumber lesson rang in my mind.

Analogies have their limits; so did this one. Even allowing myself a fair range of distortion I discovered no answers. And yet I did find the source of my emotional sounding.

Like McCumber browns, my step-kids were forever rising where I didn't expect them. For years I chased their minds about—their bodies, sometimes. More often than not I tried to entice them, casting ideas across a dinner table or couch or Dr. Seuss book. I think I played them gently, and firmly; I hope my respect showed. To this day they fill me with wonder.

"I don't get it," I've written. "I take no credit," save perhaps for never beating their spirits like f—k-dad did that day. As the time comes for their release—it has for Marc, happens soon for the twins—a mix of pride and longing confuses me. The feeling's not wholly unlike the emotion that strikes me when a fine trout leaves my hand for the world.

Sentiment, maybe sap, but every father is a fisher of sorts, and every mother—teachers, like it or not. We offer lessons at dinner, and bedtime, and buoy lines.

19

❧❦❧

I Am Curious (Tyer)

❧❦❧

I take a great deal of grief about my flies. About my fly *tying*. It happened again last week.

"Look," said my persecutor, "check in my box. Everything in there is pattern you can name."

I didn't get it. "So?"

"Like this one—what is it?"

"Breadcrust."

He looked surprised. "That's right. How about this one?"

"Royal Trude—is this a test? Or were you making a point here?"

"The point is that even you"—I *particularly* liked that qualifier—"even you can figure out what they are. Your box, on the other hand. . . ." He shook his head. "I doubt I could identify anything in there."

I almost said, "So what?" But I got it. "I rarely tie the same fly twice," I admitted.

He smirked. "No kidding."

Know that this cruel fellow is both a show and commercial tier. Worse, he knows his bugs far better than I do, and like me has vials of them at home, although his are in neat racks, while mine are strewn about my office and workshop like dead soldiers after a good party.

"But you do tie from life," I insisted.

"I adapt patterns," he replied defensively. "But I don't invent each one from scratch."

Which is, I could tell from his voice, a *bad* thing.

"Look at it this way," he said. "If I ever asked you 'What pattern are they hitting?' What would you say?"

"Well. . . ."

"Don't bother. I wouldn't have a clue."

Then he lashed me with his riding crop. Hard. Twice.

Well, no. But for two more days he ragged and nagged and gloated about this egregious character flaw. I considered having him fixed, though I knew it would be difficult to find a veterinarian at that altitude. We had an awfully good time anyway.

Yesterday, however, I was in a brooding mood and found myself staring at a tying table eight inches deep in mostly organic materials. I mean, certainly my fly "design" habits are a manifestation of something—but what, exactly? Since I find it helpful to brood with an object in hand (it just looks better—see Hamlet juggling Yorick's skull), I extracted a gray ostrich plume from a tangle of copper wire, Kevlar thread, human hair, and Flashabou. Then I struck a wistful pose. "Tomorrow and tomorrow and tomorrow, something something, struts on the stage, yada yada, and there she was just a walkin' down the street, singing do wa ditty, ditty dum, ditty day."

Clearly the plume was all wrong for such musings. Even so, you should know that gray ostrich herl is great stuff for mimicking the color and movement of gills on the underside of a salmonfly nymph's thorax. I have a specimen around here somewhere, *Pteronarcys californica*, maybe—I just call him "Phil"—and if I found it and held it up to the light, you'd see that I'm right on this one. You'd also notice a cinnamon translucence created by light passing through the abdomen. Now consider this: What if you could combine a gray ostrich gill with a body material that lets through light in just such a succulent-looking way? Add rubber legs or webby hackle—maybe both—then drop that sucker into one of the Trinity River's riffles during the *Pteronarcys* migration, tumbling it down to one of the beasts tucked in beneath the willows, a brown that will open a mouth into which your fist would fit, along your wrist clear up to your watchband. . . .

What if. . . .

That's when it struck me—an idea so important that a blow from the plume might have dropped me to my knees. Suddenly, the truth lay naked before me, writhing around a little and looking good, revealed even as I was drifting the Trinity in my mind and reaching for a chair where I might sit and bow my head to a hook again. What came to me was this:

What if . . . is such a deceptively innocent preface to speculation and wonder, ultimately an invitation to experiment. "What if" defines my approach to tying. It creates hope that I can find an answer to an interesting problem, and that hope motivates me more than the need to fill a fly box. Curiosity even supersedes a need for certainty. If I knew for sure that a size 18 Adams would raise every fish in a Sierra stream, as Stephan Haggard could demonstrate, I'd still arrive with eighteen other patterns to try. "Perhaps it's the gray they like? Probably the size. What about a size eighteen Elk Hair Caddis, then? In green? And what would they do with an Adams tied in orange? No, all in red—call it "Adam's Apple, the Trout Temptation." And I wonder if those little fish eat those giant cranefly larvae? Wonder if I can tie one up with that dirty cream iridescence. . . ."

"Inveterate tinkerer" is what people call those of us who think like that, amused that we're eager to apply such energy to trivial tasks. They also say we have "a tendency to overlook the obvious."

I grok this. But just for the record, what we inveterate tinkerers don't do—at least not all the time—is ignore the efforts of other, wiser folks, those with experience and expertise. For example, when I set out to tie a particular bug, I'll almost always check a pattern book before I start. For years, I've used Randle Stetzer's *Flies: The Best One Thousand*. Lately, I've consulted Dave Hughes's *Trout Flies*, plus *The Fly Tier's Benchside Reference* and *Trout Flies of the West*, both by Jim Schollmeyer and Ted Leeson, though I may use many others, including illustrations from retail catalogs.

The problem—or the pleasure—is that any and all of these sources will likely offer me a half-dozen approaches, or twice that many, to tying a fly much like the one I want. The designers use old and new and sometimes novel ways of applying scores of materials. They belong to exclusive schools of thought about representation, and they disagree about what fish see, what they find enticing or provoking. One ties a scud with a conspicuous carapace, another leaves the shell off completely but teases out every guard hair in the dubbing—must be a leg man. Here's a hackled emerger, here's one that uses flared deer hair, and another floated with foam, yet another with CDC. . . .

Decisions, decisions. And not just "This one or that?" Dave Hughes describes LaFontaine's Deep Sparkle Pupa, tied with Antron to represent gas bubbles under the exoskeleton, but he also admires Larry Solomon's Caddis Pupa, "which [captures] the exact shape of the natural, not the impression of the bubble of air, like LaFontaine's Sparkle Pupa."

"What I would like to see," Hughes continues, "is an experiment combining the duck-winged concept of Solomon and Leiser with the Antron Sparkle Yarn used by LaFontaine."

"Yes yes yes," say I.

Ah, but then, would anybody recognize the result in my box? What if I added a bead—glass or plastic? Copper or brass? Not in an idle way, just anywhere, in some randomly selected size or color, but smartly—get a gander of Jim Pettis's caddis series if you can, flies which make me think "Of course" every time I see them. They've surely answered his "What ifs?" on the McCloud and Sacramento, stood a guide's test over time.

"But that's the point!" I can imagine my peckish friend saying, enthusiastically pushing his clean thumbnail at a pattern beautifully built, to proper proportions, now impaled among a platoon of clones. "These have been developed over time, by people who knew what they were doing. It's not just tradition, you see. It's thoughtful evolution, and I respect that. I appreciate what's been learned, and passed on to me." Oh, yes, I can just see him, as I fabricate his dialogue, puffing up like a pigeon.

"A passenger pigeon," I would suggest with a cackle. Then I would insist, vigorously, that I am not without respect for my elders and betters. Nor do I pretend that tinkering types often invent a better Breadcrust. It's not often that a mutating cell advances the species, I know; and unreasonable innovation leads to absurd travesties, as is evidenced every year by the women's fashion industry. I tie with pleasure and indulge my imagination, but in the end, I know it's more likely that one of my friend's careful adaptations will produce something of lasting value.

He is also more in the mainstream, I suppose. Fly fishers are an orderly bunch, all in all, unusually tidy, even contained. But know this: We are also gamblers, every one. "What if?" is built into the game, fundamental. What if there's a trout beside that stone? Taking *Baetis?* What if I make this cast, mend the drift just so?

I know those "What ifs" also fascinate my friend. Like the rest of us, if he never got the right answer, he would not play; but if he always did, he'd find it too dull to bother. No matter what happens at the vise, if you even have one, every cast onto water is an inquiry—"What if?"—to which the answer is always potentially "Yes!" It is that affirmation that feels good, not the strain a fish may inflict on your forearm.

Put it this way: You can double-haul all day, but it's still a mind game.

Which is what brown trout were playing with my pal and me, not long after my flies failed muster, on a clear, high mountain lake, under thunderheads. All afternoon, bursts of rain knocked down large flying ants, which the wind sailed through slicks, lined up along scum lines and sometimes even pressed together into dark little rafts.

The browns rose steadily, selectively, as in "I've seen five legs move, if the sixth does, I'll eat it." For four hours they baffled us completely. And that, friends, is a lot of "What ifs" come to naught.

And then I thought, "What if I can't float a better ant than these thousands of others? What if the fish are too full to eat much even if I could?"

What makes a brown trout bite? Hunger. *Aggression*, especially when provoked by another fish of lesser rank, some social inferior. Like, say, like, one of last fall's more impertinent spawn.

How big would one of those babies be, exactly?

Orange. Brown. Gold.

Hey. I tied one of those. . . .

First cast. No—really. I put it right off one of those rises that had tortured us so long. Stripped twice, got *hammered*. Amazingly deep fish, for spring, beautiful. I taped him at fifteen inches.

"Good work. What'd he hit?" called my pal.

I started to speak, stopped. I looked at him a long moment. Then, very slowly, I began to smile, very broadly. "Man," I said, shaking my head with conspicuous sorrow. "Oh, man. This is so sad. I mean, if only he'd taken some fly that was, you know, tied like some pattern you have in your box. . . ."

What a good, good groan I heard, a *fine* sound, really. "Oh, all *right* then. Just tell me what it looked like, will you?"

It is for moments like this one that I carry my riding crop, a 3-weight, with great action right through the butt.

20

❧❧❧

The Broken Rod

❧❧❧

I keep all sorts of things for all sorts of reasons, most of them sentimental. Rods are particularly difficult to discard. Though I've parted with a few there remains in my closet—on my walls, and under the house where it's dry—a remarkable collection of little value to anyone but me.

Odd rods: a worn, much abused spin/fly Eagle Claw Trailmaster of yellow glass, given to me by a woman named Becky in 1974; a ten-dollar Shimano 7-weight that was as good as I needed for a very long time; a peculiar, solid wood stick, square in cross section, with a handle of several thousand hand-tied knots.

I ran across each of these the other evening and paid them scant attention. I'd just finished up at a major sportsmen's show, a long and intense affair this year, where I'd had more than my share of good fortune and enough bad—humiliating, to be blunt—that I was feeling rather put upon and dangerously angry. The rod-finding was incidental to my efforts to locate within the detritus of my office enough tackle for the first fishing trip in too long, and I was shoving things about too hard until I happened upon another rod, this one already broken.

It's a two-piece Browning Silaflex, a "Dolly Varden" the color of bourbon, with an elegant brass ferrule and simple, beautiful, black and gold wraps. As always, the sight of it startled me; but as soon as I held it in my fingers I felt a kind of stillness, something like the silence that falls upon you certain nights in the mountains when you're alone and it's so quiet the sky aches.

The break is ragged and sharp, an inch below the ferrule. There's nothing to be done for it, though parts could be salvaged—the snake guides and tip-top, the reel seat if you wanted.

That's not why I still have it. I keep this rod for the memory of two people. Fair warning: this is a true and not entirely happy story.

I'll make up names: Danny and Dolly. I met her first, on a locked ward where I then worked as a nurse. I didn't know Dolly very well. She was a client on the south station while I was assigned to the north. In a folder of mind I filed her this way: eighteen-year-old white female, brown-haired, obese, nearly mute, with a wide-eyed stare. My only vivid memory of her stay was from an incident when I found her pinned against the wall by one of our resident sociopaths, a pretty blond boy who routinely bullshitted his way out of Santa Rita Jail by manipulating needy social workers. He was leaning over her and whispering, "I'll get you, I'll get you" with such intense pleasure that he did not hear me approach.

Of course her stare was even wider than usual. But there was something else in it, something strangely *knowing*.

I met Danny two years later, at a day-treatment program where I was teaching. An alcoholic and son of an alcoholic, Danny lived with his drunken father and had for some time been trying to get both of them straight. Failing that and overwhelmed with shame, he'd cut both wrists—the wrong direction, but deep. He came to us still in bandages.

Turned out Danny was a fisherman. A serious fisherman—he had even crewed for a commercial boat, before a fire burned it to the waterline. That didn't stop him. He fished almost every night, for stripers and whatever else, casting and drinking until he was mostly drinking. Sometimes he would fall asleep on the Alameda rock wall.

"Fishing is the one thing he loves," said his treatment coordinator, "that and his father, a self-centered louse who he also hates. I was hoping you could maybe talk fishing stuff with him. See if you can get him to engage."

It didn't go well at first: Danny was also something of a paranoid personality. Not a paranoid schizophrenic—delusional, hearing voices—but one of those people whose suspicions go beyond what's reasonable. Like many paranoids, however, he desperately wanted to trust people. I was one of several he found at our program.

That was fine. I really liked him. Underneath the fear and frustration he was decent to the core, kind and proud, with a sly, generous sense of humor.

I would have fished with him if it was allowed, and did tell him about a favorite local spot. He started going there; then, when he settled into the program, he would take a couple of other clients with him, using tackle I loaned. I worried that it would be awkward if I met them some evening, but I was pleased to hear they were enjoying themselves.

I heard that from Danny. By then it was a ritual that each day he would report the evening's fishing to me; when I went fishing I would do the same. Smart angler that he was, Danny soon discovered the lair of an enormous bass—had even hooked her briefly, on a gray Rooster Tail spinner.

"Brood stock," I said when he told me about it. And because I was comfortable doing so, added, "You ought to leave her alone."

He nodded, laughed. "I will. I mean, not just because I should. She could *hurt* you."

Danny joined AA. He confessed that he loved to build rods, had been wrapping saltwater sticks for years. Eventually he brought me several to look at. One had an astonishing motif of tiny thunderbirds. He glowed when I admired it, and asked if he could wrap one for me. I reluctantly refused—clinic rules—then his treatment coordinator approached me with the same request. "He really wants to give something back. It's painful for him to always be on the receiving end and he feels so much shame anyway. Let's work something out. You pay for materials, I'll call it vocational rehab."

We did. I'd bought the old Silaflex years before at a garage sale, already stripped of guides, for a dollar. Danny was pleased with what he did to it, and I was delighted. A month later, he worked up the courage to approach a local rod maker, who gave him a commission.

Soon after, late one evening, I did see Danny at my fishing spot. He was with another client; he waved and kept his distance, watching as I nymphed up a few stockers. He was still there near dark, and whistled when a holdover rainbow took my dropper and ripped deep into my backing.

The next day in my office he asked if I would teach him something about fly fishing. I'd hoped that would happen.

It all looked good but Danny was still drinking, less often, in binges almost convulsive. "I'm afraid his father is sabotaging him," said his treatment coordinator. "And when Danny drinks now, I think he feels worse about it, hating himself for disappointing people." That was ominous, but neither of us suspected that when Danny woke from a night of transgressions he would slice into his arms with a fillet knife.

"You don't recognize me, do you?"

I laughed. I'm not oblivious to the fact that some of my clients are attractive women, just deliberately distant from that aspect; so it was a funny idea that I might forget this drop-dead pretty person, curved and lean, with live, inquiring eyes.

"No. I'm afraid I don't."

She tried to remind me, getting nowhere. That made her smile harder.

"Here's how you'll remember," she said, and described the incident with the sociopath in the hallway. I did remember then, and when I shook my head at how she'd changed, she blushed her pleasure. In the intervening time she'd found religion, in a sane sort of way, and taken up aerobics with a half-crazed obsession. She'd also finished high school at one of the alternate campuses, and had applied to our day treatment partly to structure her time before beginning her first semester at a junior college.

She seemed to have come such a long way, but I had no idea how far until a clinical review revealed that she'd been born into a notorious motorcycle gang, and that her father had begun using and passing her out as a sexual favor when she was eleven years old. This went on until that breakdown at eighteen, which got her into the hospital where I met her, from which she'd gone to a halfway house, from there out on her own.

That knowing look I'd noticed, when the sociopath had her pinned?

She loved learning, I soon found in my classes. She had a passion for ideas and craved new words.

Pretty soon she also loved Danny.

"I don't deserve her," he said one afternoon in my office, practically writhing with anxiety.

"Of course not," I answered. "You still fish bait sometimes. But that will change."

He scowled, then laughed. "Seriously."

"Seriously? For seriously, talk to your treatment coordinator. For what it's worth, though, I bet you'll feel better if you treat her as well as you possibly can. If you pay attention, she can probably show you how."

He shook his head.

But the pairing held. Together with Danny's fisher friends, the couple constructed a small clique. I saw less of Danny for that, though Dolly came to every class.

Soon I stopped seeing much of Danny at all. He started missing days at the program. When he did come in he would not take off his sunglasses, which meant he'd been drinking. On one such occasion I watched Dolly watching him as he slumped on a couch in the client's lounge. I tried to interpret her expression. She looked caring, certainly, but not histrionic. She looked patient, solid. Later, one of Danny's angling buddies told me she would not drink with him, and would leave when he got sloppy, after making it clear she would be back.

At last I lured Danny into my office, on the pretext of describing a good fishing trip. He nodded at the pictures. Behind his sunglasses I could barely see the whites of his eyes and his blue irises looked black. "You use the rod I wrapped?" he asked.

"I'm saving it."

He adjusted the glasses, his mouth a weak sneer. "Probably worthless," he said.

I said what I should and got nowhere. His treatment coordinator couldn't help; he wouldn't see her.

I did take Danny's rod fishing soon after. I even looked around for him when I got to the spot we now shared, with more than half a hope he might show. He didn't.

The Silaflex had the old line-system rating, for what I figured was a 7-weight. It moved well, with the kind of smooth, medium-action flex some wise people still like. I laid out a short cast, worked out line, and while lifting twenty or thirty feet of it off the water felt a sudden change in load even as I heard the glass crack and the rod snapped in half. Snapped, almost clear through—one part hanging to the other by a few fibers.

I sat down. I looked at the rod for a long time. I had no idea how I could explain it to Danny.

I never had to. Danny shot himself two weeks later. They say his note read like a relentless howl of remorse, a self-excoriating scream of shame. Altogether they found more than sixty knife slices on his body—thighs as well as biceps. I'd only known him four or five months, but it was one of the most difficult suicides I'd ever dealt with.

The whole staff cringed to think of what might happen to Dolly.

She stayed away two days. On the third she showed and the make-up did not quite hide the redness around her eyes. But her head was up, and her gaze level when she asked to see me. What happened went a lot like this:

She sat down in my office, looked around at all the fishing junk and pictures. She almost smiled.

"I guess it works for you," she said softly.

She was my student—or client, if you want—and I was supposed to say something reassuring, thoughts to support her spirit. I couldn't think of anything right away.

"I wish it had worked for Danny," she continued, then she asked if I'd gone fishing when I heard. I told her I had. "Did it help?"

"Not very much."

She nodded. "I've been doing aerobics for two days."

I nodded.

"It helps." She paused. "Do you know why?" She waited.

"No. No, I don't."

She smiled when she nodded. "Here's what I think: aerobics reminds me of what I can control. I can control my body. Not the things that happen to it, but how I move. How I feel about moving. It reminds me that I really am the person that I make myself into, more than anything else."

She was watching me now, wondering, I guessed, how much I knew about her past.

Enough that right then I desperately wanted to ask her how she had come through what she had, unbowed, without, so far as I could see, the kind of psychic burn scars I have so often witnessed. Once upon a time I edited a doctoral dissertation that tried to discuss why some abused children became abusers and others developed a nearly pathological desire to protect people. Of course, the results were inconclusive; but here was Dolly, a soft-eyed phoenix. What was the secret to that?

I said nothing, but noticed her gaze again. It wasn't penetrating so much as inclusive, as if she could walk away and write down everything I was wearing and the shapes of the scar tissue above my eyes. If she had no idea what question I wanted to ask, still, she suspected; and the expression she wore was much like that one I saw when she was watching Danny. There was even something of that knowing quality I'd seen on the ward.

"I came to say goodbye," she said. "Classes are starting at Chabot College."

"Right. Yes."

"I know staff people are worried about me, how I'll handle this. But I'll be okay."

"You will." I didn't mean to sound so abrupt, so awkward, but she seemed not to notice.

"Yeah." She inhaled deeply, sighed. "You see . . . maybe it doesn't seem important, but I learned something in my family that helps me a lot. . . . In the end, you're separate from other people, unless you don't want to be. No matter what, you'll be okay as long as you're the only person inside your head, because that's where things can hurt you most, or make you feel better. The most important thing is to keep your *mind* to yourself." She hesitated. "Do you know what I mean?"

"I think so."

"Yeah? Because that's why I felt so bad for Danny, you know? My family didn't care what happened in my head, so they left that part of me alone. But Danny's father. . . . It's different, what he does. What he did."

She shook her head and for a moment seemed to lose herself in thought, touching the tips of her fingers together, pressing, concentrating.

This lasted less than a minute, not half that, I suppose. Then she looked around the room, taking it in again. "When you're fishing," she said slowly, and the phrase began a question, "that's all you're thinking about, isn't it? Nothing else?"

"Yes. Yes, usually."

"Yeah. That's what Danny wanted, tried to make happen—and sometimes it did, I think. But not for very long, or long enough. Danny always had his father in his head. No matter what, there was his father, at the back of his mind, in the bottom of every bottle." She shook her head.

I was still thinking about that when she stood up.

"I have to go," she said gently.

"Right."

"But before I do, there's one other thing. Danny . . . Danny would have wanted you to have his fishing tackle. I told his father that, but he said he wants to keep it to remember Danny by." She shook her head, smiling. "He's going to sell it for booze. But Danny, he would have wanted you to get it. He can't help it that you won't."

"Of course."

Her face brightened suddenly. "But at least you have that rod he made for you, right?"

I looked at her. "Right. Absolutely."

I have beautiful wraps on a broken shaft. I have the story of that rod in my head, and written now. Maybe it's not a parable for all time, but it's mine when I need it.

I needed it that day after the show, smoldering, unable to escape feelings about a situation in which dirty things happened for ugly reasons and the parties who profited put my name to the acts. In time, many people would learn what actually happened; others might wonder, perhaps offer the benefit of doubt; and some, for good reason, would assume the worst.

That bothered me enough that it was important to remember Dolly's lesson, and Danny's—both sides of the same idea—that shame is so dangerous that you had better choose when you feel it.

I did go fishing, at last. I tried to think only about the rod, my line, flies and casts, hopes. It wasn't easy. For many hours I wondered if I wasn't more like Danny than I wanted to be.

Early in the afternoon big fish began to midge. A breeze came up, but they continued, raising swirls of nervous water in the ruffled surface.

I borrowed a canoe and paddled way upwind, picked a drift. I kept the line ready and watched, turning and turning. It was difficult, nearly impossible, to predict a fish's course—to anticipate, make throws from awkward positions, mend for wind and the speed of my sailing. In three hours of paddling up and drifting down I cast maybe forty times. I landed six fish, good ones, on a size 20 pupa, missing only two strikes that I saw.

All that time I was alone in my head. That night, camped by the lake and huddled up, I read by the light of a Coleman lantern, a new book about stripers by George Reiger. He must have lived right down the street from my basement in Berkeley, starving to write, just as I would ten years later. He tells stories of the men and fish he once knew.

Fifty pages in I discovered that Reiger had entered my head; he was welcome. I paused to appreciate that, then realized how many friends visit my mind so often they might as well own property there, near to the great estate of my own father, who smiles at me from shadows.

For a moment the sky ached with silence. When I returned to my thoughts I was wry: many people I let into my mind would tease me, if ever they realized the grand clutter of my thoughts.

But then, I suppose I could just tell them that I keep there all sorts of things, for all sorts of reasons.

21

Second Hands

New. So many people delight in objects they obtain in mint condition, unsoiled and unsullied and still in the shrink-wrap. Deranged sorts love to inhale that "new car smell," which I'm pretty sure emanates from complex plastic molecules way too hazardous to test on lab rats. But here's the brutal fact: aficionados of virgin goods appreciate a state of being which is only an instant away from that first scratch, prick, dent, or indelible stain.

Still, new is important, as anybody in industry will tell you. Any industry. Ours, for instance: recently I attended a fly-tackle show where were collected the smoothest-running reels, strongest and most subtle rods, finest commercial flies, and acres of softgoods sewn so cleverly that I expect soon to see a wallet which folds out into a raincoat or float tube—your choice! In this chapped hand I held a pair of pliers that cost more than I'm asking for a 1985 Honda Accord with good tires, a fair body, and less than

150,000 miles (see classifieds). I saw saltwater streamers tied from fibers reflecting colors first seen by Timothy Leary, so shiny that magpies will commit suicide against your window trying to get to your vise. I found hooks that could pierce Kevlar armor; shirts cut from fabrics that block harmful sunlight, wick away sweat, repel rain and release irresistible pheromones; fly lines that part the wind, turn invisible, sink like steel cable or float forever; hats that expand in many directions, then contract to the size of your fist. And just as I got used to the idea of truly comfortable waders that "breathe," here comes an "oil-impregnated belt" which suggests that some cow suffered terrible indignities.

Tackle-R-Us, it was. Don't suppose for a minute I didn't enjoy seeing every bit of it. And don't imagine that I will take cheap shots like "if only people would learn to cast, read water, present well." While a few of these products are mostly packaging, others represent genuine innovation of one kind or another; I was fascinated more than once by an ingenious idea. If I got sulky about prices, that's no big thing, because like most writers I know where to sell blood.

So what did I get, what did I get, what did I get?

Thought you'd never ask: several tippet spools of a new fluorocarbon, eight hooks, and a water filter. I begged a fly line, arranged to borrow a rod for a trip and, maybe, buy a replacement jaw for a vise. I almost forked out for a stripping basket; I shook hands on a TBA trade of a collectible book for a blemished reel and accepted two more books because reviewing them is a job of mine. Reluctantly I routed other offers of neat objects to product testers who can promote in print the stuff they like.

That's *it*, you say?

I picked up a little something for a woman's birthday, and bought Sophie four pewter pins, one each of a trout, bat, orca, and salamander. I would have got Max a present, but so far he likes best trucks and animals, books showing trucks and animals, and the large cardboard boxes I get from Easton Aluminum, on which he stands, dances, sings, and vigorously draws colored lines. (Note that he already has two Easton boxes—no sense spoiling the boy.)

And?

From friends, I picked up a pair of used saltwater reels and a 10-weight one of them built a while back.

Say *what?* You say. Surrounded by all this new, new, new tackle, which you confess that you liked and admired . . . ?

Perhaps because I grew up without older siblings, the idea of hand-me-downs never bothered me a bit—quite the opposite. I prowled my father's closet and scavenged in his bureau, workshop, and tool shed, keen to someday wear a 1930s-era corduroy coat (which took me clear through college), carve with his homely wood-handled "electrician's knife" (now on my desk), and slice either sheet metal or mulberry twigs with the massive blue-steel shears which now hang on a pegboard on my workshop wall, beside his chisels, not far from his hammer and two saws. (I also coveted my mother's fountain-pen collection as far back as I can remember, but kept away from these jewels, knowing how quickly I would lose any I "borrowed," and understanding that this would lead to Arizona's first Inquisition.)

Obviously there's sentiment involved here. As there was also when I got the odd lot of clothing from one of my older or bigger pals—a rare but treasured gift, since most of them had little brothers. The overarching effect was that "second hand" never equated with "second best": in fact, when I was green, wearing Levi's right off the rack was no pleasure—stiff and way too blue—but a pair beaten soft and maybe already patched at the knees—now those were worth having, special.

Rather like the Fin-Nors I brought back from the show. These belonged to Bill and Kate Howe; and if this Ahab isn't the reel Kate used to land some record sailfish, it's certainly familiar to her hand. The Howes are big on maintenance, so the drags do their jobs and the brass housings gleam; but sure enough there's the odd nick or two to suggest "been someplace, done something—not exactly my first time, Babycakes." Bill built the rod, probably back when they were living down near San Diego, and it makes me grin to imagine those meaty fingers wrapping thread and brushing on epoxy—all this fine motor control living in digits not quite so large as kielbasa. (I did see one of those fingers crushed once, and the inside looks just like beef.)

Yep. And I'll think of the Howes every time I use these things.

I like that. For similar reasons, I like a curious 7-weight now out on loan to Tom Hnizdor, of B-17 Flies. The handle is ergonomic, looks like a better-made cork version of something they used to make for casting rods; it's called a Maniform Grip. A pair of English anglers developed it to minimize and modify the strain casting puts on tendons. One of them is David Stocker, who fourteen years ago gave me a tour of London tackle shops, merely by way of doing a kindness to a fellow fly fisher who'd come over for a wedding. David and I have kept contact since then: five years ago, he and an engineer pal, John Newton, started making Maniforms; and in 1996 I tried one out, when my family and I stayed with him in the Lake Country. Soon after, I started loaning rods built with Maniforms from my own booth at one of the trade shows, which prompted John to insist I keep one, a lovely 5-weight built on a Loomis blank.

When I broke the top section I asked Dick Galli, a rod builder, engineer, and longtime party-boat skipper out of Emeryville Sportfishing, to wrap me a new piece. The Maniform intrigued him, so I sent him a couple to play with, which caused him to one day put one on a long blank he thought I might like.

I did. So how did Thom get the rod?

I met Thom at a San Mateo show some years back, when I admired his flies. Turns out we both have nasty cases of tendinitis, so when he found a trick device that worked for him, he sent me one. When I realized the Maniform might let him get back to fishing his Michigan streams. . . .

Like that.

And like this: I also have a sweet sonnet of a fiberglass 4-weight made by Mario Wojniki, because Lisa Owings knows that her husband Jeff loves rods—especially Mario's. "Which one would he really like?" she whispers every year before the Grizzly Peak Fly Fisher's auction. And every year, Jeff looks stunned when Lisa outbids somebody. One night she bought him a Mario rod he wanted more than another Mario rod rather like it, which he already owned; and when Jeff wanted to painlessly finance a little trip, he phoned me, wondering if . . . ?

I fish an Ascent reel on the Mario because I like it, and because Chip Flor, its designer, used to share a booth with Jim Scherer and me at the International Fly Tackle Dealer Show, in Denver, before Chip went on to engineer reels for Loomis. I also had the honor of injuring an early prototype of this model when, while petting a large and affectionate gelding beside a ranch pond, I spotted an enormous rainbow cruising along the bank toward where we stood. So madly did I strip line for a cast that I tripped a mechanism—said Flor later, "I never *imagined* anyone would treat *any* reel like that"—which caused the spool to spin free at the very moment I dotted the trout's eyes with a scud. The fish took, hooked itself, felt steel and lunged as the loose line tangled insanely and the rod ripped forward even as the affectionate gelding, eager for more attention, grabbed a mouthful of my hair and yanked back—

Only the tippet snapped. I staggered around laughing until I got moist.

It's all personal, in other words. Which isn't exactly the same kind of appreciation collectors enjoy, people who thrill to think that Elvis fished this 6-weight; theirs is a world I don't know much about. But having a sense that an object played some part in a life I appreciate; that's *fine*. It adds a corporeal form to a fond feeling or funny memory, represents it in three dimensions, with weight, contours and a purpose our fingers share. Given a choice between a trout reel machined to micro-tolerances, or one banged back into working order after a fall using the butt end of a Buck knife while a pal steadied the project on a gleaming piece of East Sierra granite, which all led to catching those goldens brilliant as the sun setting on a Fabergé egg. . . .

Given that kind of satisfaction, do I mind if a friend's palm left sweat on the cork of a rod grip?

Well then, you might wonder, does that mean I am eager to give away objects of mine?

No, I just realized. For one thing, I don't imagine that everybody else's attitude resembles mine. For another, I tend to beat things to death—it's not only cars I push through decades, but also favorite shirts, leather cases, knives, and bench grinders. And I don't do this carefully: I am a negligent owner, cavalier and lazy. I treasure, but do not pamper. If I fix most of what I break—and even feel that I've made a tool more mine by putting it back together—I'm not above duct-tape solutions, and last month I successfully mended a leaking toilet by wiring into place a cleat wrench used on golf shoes.

Which is by way of saying that there's usually not much left when I'm done. Getting my hand-me-downs could be confusing. ("Oh that's so nice, thank you . . . what is it, exactly?") Perhaps on some level I even accept the idea that I'm a last stop for certain items other people loved first, when new—products they might once have happily carried home from a show.

And finally, I confess that the only things of mine I really hope will last awhile, and hold values, are my children and a little bit of writing. Each kid is a first, new every day; the words are about what I'm worth.

Perhaps that's why I like signing books, putting my hand to something that will rest in someone else's. Aren't essays and reflections the best leftovers of our lives? To leave a few stories and a little laughter—perhaps memories of something we're proud we made, by ourselves or as part of a good crew. . . .

It's hard to shrink-wrap the kind of things that matter most to me, I've discovered. On the occasions I've tried, the results were always the same: the kids say it makes them feel "clammy."

22

Fishing the Baja Loca

Ron Vander Heiden rises to the surface of the sea, sputtering, laughing, swinging his head around to fling wet hair from his eyes. I watch him only an instant, but hear him cry, "Did you see that?"

I did—a smash missed as a wave buried him. Ron's already stung six or eight fish because this tube fly he has tied, an articulated squid, is performing as well in the surf as it has over three days fishing offshore in cruisers and super-*pangas*.

I'd like to congratulate Ron about that. After all, he's not only an EMT tech and Powell Rod consultant, but also the man who at this moment most reminds me of a gloriously happy golden retriever. But to open my mouth would risk swallowing the trailing edge of the wave that swamped him and now rushes me; so instead I work the forward stroke of a false cast while watching the water rise and, beyond it, a trio of dark shapes charging in from my right. Tiny surf bulls, deep-headed and -bodied, they look almost black in the gloaming, save when their dorsal fins break the surface—absurdly tall, cobalt blue, frilly.

Backcast. The water around my legs draws forward as the wave rises above my eye level. Forward cast.

I hear Ron yell "Whooooaa."

Whump.

Tons of water mute his voice while lifting me clear of the sand, pushing upward and back, rolling over my head with a dim slopping sound. I open my eyes into diffuse emerald light—an ocean of Oz—even as I still see in memory the loop of my line in flight, unfolding against the sky.

Destination: roosterfish. Reception: unknown.

I'll find out soon enough. But for some tiny piece of time I am weightless, warm, floating, so instantly relaxed that muscles in my neck and shoulder seem to surrender, letting loose that marginal organization that distinguishes tissue from its seawater source.

It's a kind of body sigh, I suppose, with a smile.

I drift down, shorts ballooning around my thighs as I hear the wave curl and crash behind me. My feet touch sand, dig for traction as my face and arm bust into air. I feel then a steady pull against the fly line. It's the suck of retreating sea, which seems to have a sound track.

"Roosters! Roosters," Ron cries, and lets loose a sustained giggle that's part shriek.

Unless that's me making that sound.

Strip strip. Strip strip.

There. I see the three descending through the face of a plunging wave; then, ahead of them, glimpse the white dash of my fly. One shape outraces the others, and in a blink changes direction. I hurl myself backwards and am simultaneously yanked forward at the waist. "You got him!" Ron shouts as the butt of the borrowed 11-weight slams into my ribs. "You got him!"

That gross grunting sound means Yes I know.

And then. . . .

See the roosterfish run. Oh, oh, oh, see him run! He is crossing the Sea of Cortez! I am running after the roosterfish! Into the ocean, I am running. Stop, roosterfish, stop! Stop-and-I-will-feed-you-stupid-dog-Spot!

I cannot begin to bring the fish back toward me, so settle for bending his route south ten or twelve degrees. Like Ron, I am laughing and making foolish sounds.

Giggling again, if you insist.

Baja, East Cape, thirty miles above Cabo San Lucas. It's been twenty-five years since the last time I visited this peninsula, and that was to camp on a *playa* just south of Ensenada and hundreds of miles north of here. Those memories should feel older than they do.

From north came the wind today, and yesterday, and the day before. None of the kind folks at Hotel Punta Colorada can remember an October when it blew so strongly. It herds long swells before it and whips up whitecaps that spark sunlight all the way to the horizon. In odd moments I smell desert—not exactly the Mojave scents I was born to, but similar, like the smells of a familiar food now baked instead of grilled.

I am burned a little, a pleasing pink, no doubt, and bruised from riding a cruiser that pitched and yawed and took the waves in its teeth and occasionally let them crash into ours. How stoic we all stayed, how steadfast, pretending to look good in order not to sour the day for others we presumed felt better. Not macho, just mannerly.

"How you doing?" someone would ask.

"Fine," would come the answer. Then, because sticking to a single syllable seemed wise, "You?"

John Ryzanych looked all right though, our first day out, as he tended the teasers he'd set, a pattern including

"Clones" and squids and a super-realistic flying fish with hinged plastic wings. John is one of our small group's experts, the fellow who organized this trip using Fishabout Outfitters, and who has guided for an outfit down the beach. He's arranging my first ever turn "in the chair," shooting for billfish with a fly rod.

For an hour I have less to do than a bus rider, who might recognize the diesel fumes that sometimes eddy behind the cabin, slowly greasing my throat. Meanwhile, the midday sun has beaten the sky flat, so I stare at the bubble trails of our baits, slowly beginning to drift and doze, perchance to dream.

Suddenly, for no reason I can fathom, I am startled alert. What? I think, almost saying it aloud. What?

Bubbles. Wakes. Far away a needlefish leaps in a perfect arc. Nothing else—yet I am taut, truly alarmed. What? What changed?

"Something," John says.

Then we see the bill slashing up through the surface to carve the lure's wake. The sail fin snaps erect, a leading edge of dorsal thrusting twenty inches clear of the water.

"*Vela vela vela!*"

John shouts, "There!" and in an orderly frenzy begins to clear rods and drag close the teaser while barking orders at a deckhand who has never played this game with a fly rod. I am yelling something also—babbling, I suspect—leaning forward, eyes flicking back and forth between the coils of 15-weight fly line at my feet and the sailfish as he pursues his attack. In my palm lies a fly the size and color of a psychedelic bluejay, its foam head trailing Mylar and Flashabou. John has told me what do—wait, wait—and warned that I will have only one cast, a kind of roundhouse throw.

"Now!"

Right. A box kite would be more aerodynamic, but the fly is out of my hand, airborne, in flight and on schedule, working in concert with everything else—boat, and wind, and John ripping the teaser still closer—so that it falls where he told me it should, ahead and to the right of the bill. Still the sailfish follows the Clone, slashing madly—smashing off a piece of the plastic, we will discover. Now I remember that I am to—

"Pop! Pop it! Pop!"

—pop the line with my hand, walking the dog as it were, taunting the fish to—

—turn!—

"Yes!"

"Fish on! Fish on!"

Fish *up*—soaring, twisting, a blue scream of movement deep blue against aqua. His fall slams a sheet of water from which he leaps, drops, dances up on his tail in the foam. For ten seconds he streaks away, eighty feet, maybe a hundred, then he launches again, leaping higher still for the speed he's gained, his body a glistening slab. For such a long instant he seems oblivious to gravity and I think *impala*, then realize he is impala-sized, five or six feet long, slender and sharp all over—bill, pectoral and dorsal spines, with tail fins like twin scimitars.

Another run, then up again. I'm still not sure I have registered his weight, nor felt the pull he might exert, because the line cannot seem to catch up to him, to connect us directly. Even so, I begin to believe I am winning, will win this battle with the wildest acrobat I can imagine.

Hubris.

Then he's pulling almost straight away and I am staring along his back as he jumps, directly down the plane of his body, close enough that I see the tail seem to bow, hesitate—

"Wrapped!" cries John.

—flexes straight—

And gone.

"Tail wrapped! Tail wrapped. . . ."

I stare after my *vela*. I am grinning. No regret shadows the glory of this fish, nor dims the images left to me. So that's what it's about, I'm thinking. How about that.

"Eight and a half minutes, you had him on," says John.

"Cool," I say. "That was so cool."

An hour later John ties into and boats a wahoo, which looks like the bastard spawn of a barracuda and tuna; then good Dr. Aric Ludvig jumps a sail that splits. We hit another *dorado*, perhaps our eighth or ninth. Meanwhile, fishing inshore in a super-*panga*, Ron and Dave Hickson, angler extraordinaire, are cracking jacks, and roosters, pompano, ladyfish, and *cabrillo*. For twenty minutes, Dave works out a marlin he guesses at between 200 and 300 pounds.

That was the first day.

That night we tied flies in the hotel's great room, after an enormous meal that began with the bar's excellent *ceviche* washed down with margaritas and vodka tonics. We ate out on the patio perched high on a bluff, proceeding to grilled *dorado* and fries, vegetables, salad, finishing with flan. It's 55 dollars a night here, on the plan we bought, but just because that includes three meals a day doesn't mean the lovely Maria skimps—not a bit. Nor did the air conditioning in our room ever cut out; and everything everywhere was clean.

Four days we spend in boats, alternating between modern cruisers and super-*pangas*. These are part of the hotel's large fleet, geared for meat-fishing conventional anglers. A few of those boys will still club an eight-foot, inedible sailfish, in order to hang it by the tail for a picture, presumably because they failed to get results from those tubular pumps advertised in the back of men's magazines. But most are a pleasant lot, friendly, and curious about our tackle and techniques. Several have even brought fly rods, though they seem inclined to treat them as rarified tools, something to try if there's an eclipse of the sun. "You landed *dorado* with those things?" "He fought a marlin?" The cruiser captain with whom we sail keeps his own counsel, which is probably for the best, for while we kill several fish, we release most; and for those we free he cannot fly signal flags, the boat's bragging right. Seems like that's a system they could easily adapt, *si?*

Banner days, are these at sea, even when the north wind blows out the bait and we must work for fish. But for three more days we cast from the beaches and rocks, and have a ball. Jacks and more jacks—several kinds; elegant pompano; queer cornet fish three feet long and five pounds. Nineteen species of fish, we count altogether, not including the sail and marlin. We even hit a rare school of black snook, landing almost a score. And always, there's the chance of roosters, small or large. Most of ours are under five pounds, though two of Dave's hit the low teens; but we see monsters in the surf, break off several mystery fish; and on the wall of the hotel dining room hangs a specimen which, given wheels, could be driven in a Soap-Box Derby. The bigger fish we glimpse mostly in the hours of low sun, but in one or two places we take fish all day.

And all the days are bright, save one.

At least, I remember it as darker. We had borrowed a car to visit a small town several miles from the hotel, where Doctor Aric lived for some part of his interesting and wayward youth. From there we drove to an estuary he thought we ought to visit, a short walk in from an apparently abandoned campground. The fishing was only fair by the standard of other days, and we were hiking back to the car when the *federales* came out of the trees.

It was a well-armed patrol. I think there were seven or eight. They watched us carefully as we approached, their faces neither hostile nor friendly, perhaps mildly interested. The story is that many of these soldiers come from the poorest ranks of society, that they are paid little, that they must literally forage on their own for supplies in the areas to which they are assigned. The story also suggests that they will on occasion act as if a law unto themselves.

Which brings to my mind, at that moment, the issue of the fishing licenses we don't have, because there were none to be found. In theory—that is, according to the good folks at Punta Colorada—if ever asked we should simply suggest that we had tried to buy them. . . .

But then, we never expected to be asked.

We never were. The soldiers passed without making any gesture more officious than a nod.

End of incident, beginning of memory:

Baja, twenty-five years ago, on that *playa* just south of Ensenada, end of spring break from a college in southern California. Two friends and I left a man on a gray Baja beach. I don't know who he was; I'm not even certain how he sustained injuries so horrible that there's really no point to describing them, save to say that on first seeing him, and hearing the sounds he made, I thought simply, "I hope he dies."

We had not wanted to leave him. But twelve or fifteen members of a Mexican motorcycle gang with whom we had earlier skirmished—when there had been an almost equal number of us—made a convincing argument. I even

suspect the one who gave the order "You go now" was acting in our behalf.

We drove to a cantina nearby, the only occupied
structure we knew how to find. The proprietor stared at us
as we tried in English and Spanish to get help: "Policia.
Policia. Ambulencia."

After half a minute he pointed to a shelf on which
stood one bottle of Pepsi and another of Dos Equis. "That
is for you," he said clearly and disdainfully. "Only that."

It had been a gray day, then, one of the very worst of many
since that convince me almost anything can happen at
any time. I mull that over as we drive back to our clean
and friendly hotel, where you can't actually lock your
room door, and don't need to. Certainly I had lived in
more dangerous places since—and do today, because most
places contain more threats than Baja; and very, very few
feel as safe as Punta Colorada. So why did I let that incident keep me away for so long? The awfulness of the
wounds I saw? Our helplessness? Or something else entirely?

It's tempting to speculate. For lack of another explanation, I toy with an idea, or maybe a worldview, that
includes both the inevitability of consequence and the
arbitrary nature of tragedy. Perhaps it's just that contrasts
in Baja are so stark, between a hard, scorched-looking
land and this lovely sea, balmy and blue and alive.

I don't know.

Over and over again Ron and I pound surf and are
pounded. We fish for hours, long after we've turned wrinkled and pink. Dave tries to join us, but he is too svelte—a
wave just picks him up and deposits him up the beach,
then leaves him to drip, which is also something worth

giggling about. So Dave goes back to whacking pompano and jacks at the corner where beach meets rocks, before sitting beneath a *palapa* to split a beer with John. Then the two of them, according to all their reports, laugh at Ron and me as we romp about taking water and roosters and acting like children or puppies or fly fishers having a pretty good time in the sun.

23

Of Bass and Sociopaths; or, I Was a Second-Grade Panfish

In late summer the hills of Alisal are the color of lions and roll away from the lake like waves. Giant cottonwoods shade the banks of a brilliant blue lake there, and I searched shadows as our boat drifted into the soft hours of evening.

"He could be out there," I whispered *sotto voce*.

"Who?" Dan Gracia asked innocently, even as he thumbed back the lip of yet another foot-long bass. The fish were moving up from the edges now, hunting. This one took a popper tossed right up against tulles.

"Him. Jack Ellis."

"The writer?"

I nodded. "He haunts me."

"Really? Jack Ellis?"

"Oh yes. So far, only in spirit. But I'm waiting."

Lydia's boat edged out from the next cove over. "How you guys doing?"

Dan waved. "Great! How about you?"

She held up her hand with the five fingers spread apart, closed the hand, opened it again. Dan applauded. Lydia laughed, took a quick bow. "But no picture fish yet?" she asked. "Shoot. If only you'd been here last week." She laughed. "Or next week, probably."

A cruel one, is Lydia Goodhue, Lake Manager at Alisal, a posh and successful dude ranch two hours north of L.A., where frazzled urbanites and families can select from programs offering horseback riding, golf, tennis, and a variety of other activities all sandwiched between gourmet meals. The 100-acre lake has always been a popular picnic destination; in recent years Dan has directed Orvis fly-fishing schools there. Alisal was his suggestion, when I told him I'd been asked to write a piece on West Coast bass.

I agreed, but with some trepidation. There's a *quid pro quo* implicit in such invitations, the understanding that if a writer gets the story he hopes for, the lodge, guide or outfitter will receive due credit. Therein lay my problem: I didn't need just bass, but a behemoth. Not the one-, two-, or three-pounders that make for wonderful sport, but a fish that ate mallards and beaver pups and was a danger to pedestrians.

"I think they've had a twelve-pounder," Dan had said. "But I'm not sure it was caught on a fly."

That was the other rub—and where the author of *Bassin' with a Fly Rod* came in. "Ellis just doesn't think big bass are really a fly-rod fish," I advised Dan glumly. "He likes them small and medium sized, because they come to the top, cruise mid-depths; they're active and aggressive. But he thinks the big ones are slugs. He says they get fat, lose their looks, and just hang around in heavy cover, waiting in ambush. Kind of like old Hells Angels who've retired to a wet bar outside Modesto."

"What?"

"Yeah. Ellis says he caught an eleven-pounder accidentally, and it was so grotesque he wouldn't even take its picture."

Dan laughed. " 'Accidentally'?"

"I believe he meant while fishing for smaller, more exciting bass. But it's always possible he was wading and got the fish stuck on his zipper."

Dan seemed disinclined to consider this possibility. "What if you wrote about how much fun smaller bass are to catch?"

"Oh Dan," I said, shaking my head sadly. "Big bass are special. Let me explain this to you. . . ."

Growing up in Arizona, I learned that "largemouths" were the fish that mattered. I pursued them on hundreds of expeditions that typically ended with a bucketful of live bluegills I'd haul home to our patio pond. Once in a while I did get a baby bass, but these were usually smaller than the tin medallions my father and I wore on our black velvet Indian Guides shirts to represent our Walipai names: I was "Leaping Bass" and Dad was—to my infinite annoyance—"Sleeping Bass." In fact, brute "hawgs" were almost as rare as javelina, and I'd only seen the hind ends of those. But I did know first-hand that lunkers lurked in the neighborhoods I fished, because about every other year I'd be reeling in another little 'gill and feel, suddenly, a sickening tug. Then, for the five seconds it might take for the big bass to disgorge, I'd have a sense of what battling one might be like.

Shocking incidents. Since a bass's teeth don't cut much, my accidental bluegill baits would survive these assaults, and I didn't like the expression I read in their eyes when I finally landed them. They made me think of Jonah and Pinocchio's dad. That wasn't the only anthropomorphizing I indulged: in second grade it occurred to me that my buddies and I were ourselves rather like panfish—quick, smallish sorts hanging about in schools during recess—and that big bass resembled the frightening eighth-grade bullies who lurked at the edge of our playground, bored thugs who really would hurt you.

In an adult word, then, bass were sociopaths.

"Sociopaths?" repeated Lydia, with the kind of light laugh well-balanced folks reserve for the musings of people like me. "A fish?"

I glared at her across the elegantly set table of the Alisal dining hall, where we had eventually retreated to continue discussion of the species. "You would not be so amused, young lady," I said, gesturing with a fork on which was impaled a piece of rightly roasted beef, "if you were a frog."

"I won't argue that," she said generously.

"Or a bat," I added with emphasis, already on my way into another long story which would involve a lot of semaphore, a nearly lost art.

First this note: The world-record bass lives within 100 miles of my house, in Oakland, California. Until last year, that fact was only speculation and I was a Cassandra, one of many perhaps, hawking the idea that what's sometimes called "the million-dollar fish" must be a Florida-strain largemouth living high on a diet of stocked trout—the kind of put-and-take rainbows planted by the hundreds of thousands in California's lowland waters. Lake Castaic is the place many experts expect to produce the honor, but I'd bet as quickly on several Northern California impoundments, nutrient rich, in which Floridas have now had enough time to develop. And to learn, as bass will, that the commotion produced by a hatchery truck dropping a stunned load means "Dumb-as-dirt dinner, coming up."

Proof almost positive: Last year, in a smallish lake of this sort somewhere around Santa Rosa, an angler used an eleven-inch trout-shaped lure to land, weigh—on an unofficial scale found accurate, I understand—and then release a twenty-four-pound largemouth.

Twenty-four pounds. I should think that bass was almost the size of one I met in small suburban park pond I used to fish after work, when he rose up beside my float tube to see if any part of me might be chewed loose.

How big was he, you say?

She, more likely. At a distance of four feet I had to triangulate objects to estimate her length: say a yard long. Big enough that only pride kept me from getting out of the water. No, I did not hook it. Nor did I ever hook in that place any bass over a pound. But late one evening, I whacked a bat with a false cast, which fell to the water and fluttered.

Doesn't take a prophet to see where this goes. But wait: remember those full-page black-and-white ads in the outdoor magazines, circa 1966? "An artist's conception of the Vibrobat lure"? Those hundreds of concentric lines expanding out across the page?

Three times, I pushed that bat up onto the beach with the butt of my rod. Three times, he flopped back into the water; and at last he got himself up into the black shadow beside a little dock, where a hole opened for him in the dark water, a pit not quite so large as your standard utility sink.

"—the Gaping Maw of Bat Destiny," I advised Lydia and Dan, "and for the next hour, I tell you, all I was missing was Chicken Little's commentary."

My colleagues were satisfyingly silent. They actually looked mesmerized, contemplating the possibilities. Then

Lydia hummed softly, "The *crème brûlée* is excellent, and I can personally recommend our oatmeal pie."

A stomach flu struck Dan that night in our bungalow, some intestinal equivalent of Ebola, so Lydia and I went it alone early the next morning, launching into mist. We plumbed the weed lines, and took several hefty fourteen-inch fish—"terriers," as I'd come to call them, for the way they shook their heads when they leaped. It was great fun, frankly; so it was with reluctance I at last suggested that I should soon deliver home the empty husk of poor Dan.

Lydia sighed. "I didn't want to do this," she said, sliding from beneath her seat a conventional casting outfit rigged with a deep-running chartreuse crankbait. "But this point has been so productive lately . . . I mean, I could *show* you one of the bigger fish."

"And what do your people call that tool?" I asked pleasantly.

"I know. It's not a fly rod. But—"

"Will it make the boat go faster?" I asked. *"Is it used to herd cattle?"*

"Just a couple of casts," she pleaded.

The first, it turned out, produced the biggest bass I'd seen so far, not my cover shot, but a juicy eighteen-incher. The way I figured it, he weighed about as much as The Fly Fisher's Burden.

And such distances we must carry it: I took so many trips in pursuit of my big bass I named my float tube Quahog and christened my Burk's V-Worm "Is-a-meal." In the spring I fished Big Bluff Ranch, where I arrived late one night and slept peacefully in a cabin on the water, waking to feel in my bones the drop in barometric pressure as a storm chilled the bass fishing, forcing me to settle for imitating a hatch of tiny *Caenis* that brought to the surface trout to 20 inches—woe, O woe. Then came a pond in the foothills near Grass Valley, fishing with my friend Denis Pierce. His hand-carved fly-rod plugs pulled up fish after thrilling fish, but never a lunker, unless you count one enormous bluegill that pretended to be a permit. In another small lake I worked a streamer on a Slime Line, swimming it along drop-offs where the faint green of deep weeds gave way to real depths. Eleven inchers. Foot-longs. Finally I got one half again that length; but some wormer nearby got a six-pounder, though I could tell from watching him land the fish that he was an indifferent dancer who could not hit long irons, and with lips like those would never play trombone.

In another pond I stuck fish a third that size, stalking them from cover on a sloping bank, tossing one of Ton Hnizdor's leather-legged frogs. Every time my presentation was halfway well done, a bass would explode on the fly so quickly it looked like I'd thrown a cherry bomb. I took five before I ran out of shoreline.

No danger of that on the Sacramento Delta, where 1,500 miles of tangled waterways host at least one bass for every honest American angler. And where, on July Fourth, I saw a half-dozen handsome fish while walking a fifty-yard stretch of riprap along one of the marinas. Every single one of these held a position two feet off the hot rocks, staring at the shore as if they expected visitors, maybe crawdads.

"Folks always try for them, once," laughed one of the boat owners, who then left ajar a gangway gate. Two minutes later I stood on a floating dock to cast a Woolhead Sculpin right up onto a bankside boulder. I watched the bass watch the fly as it crawled . . . so . . . slowly . . . into the water.

Got 'im. Three pounds.

"Waiting on the tide," said Leo Gutterres about those bass, when I described this phenomenon. "For crayfish that crawl up the rocks with the rising water, then must come down when the water falls. The fish know about that."

Gutterres is a much-admired California carver of bass poppers so elegant they rarely get fished—much to Leo's chagrin. I'd first spoken to him after a presentation on bass he did for the Grizzly Peak Fly Fishing Club, in Kensington, California. Six months later he let a little major surgery interfere with a bass outing on which I'd hoped to tag along, so now spoke to me during convalescence, which I had the feeling he was rushing in order to get back to the fish. I'd asked him also about the size of bass that he thought a fly fisher should hope to find. "I can tell you this," he said with gentle conviction. "That a six-pound northern black bass, on a fly rod . . . that is a fine fish. A trophy fish, in my opinion."

There we had it.

Less than a week after I talked to Gutterres, on a Saturday so windy that I could keep fifty feet of line lashing about in the air simply by lifting my rod high, as both light and temperature fell I watched a pair of beaver making late runs along a lee shore. Neither one apparently feared bass attack. Long after I'd surrendered most hope of a beast, but still played puppeteer with one of the tiny plugs I'd filched from Denis, I took the fish I'd been looking for all along, or should have been, if only I'd believed. Nearly as big as Lydia's, around the same size as the one I tricked by walking a sculpin off the riprap—two and a half, maybe three pounds. It fought quite deep and surprisingly far out into open water, then held still for an idiot camera portrait.

I was happy. And at peace.

My serenity almost survived the test: "Thirteen pounds, maybe fifteen—what a bass," said my friend Gary

Azevedo, the best micro-nymph fisher I know. "I had to call. I even got pictures."

"Incredible. Fantastic. On what fly?"

Long pause. "Fly? Oh, man. I wish. For those big ones, you got to use plastics. It's about the only way."

I let the silence build between us, hoping he'd come clean on his own. Then, "Gary. You're working for Jack Ellis, *are you not?*"

24

✦✦✦

Just Do It
and the Nike Fly Tyer

✦✦✦

One of my favorite stories
begins with a ten-year-old listening to his mother play the
piano. Newly educated in music and sharper than a serpent's tooth, this son says, "You really do play badly, don't
you, Mom?"

Mom turns, pauses and—sweetly, sweetly—answers,
"Yes, dear. And I've enjoyed playing the piano badly for
almost thirty years now."

Someday I hope to have enjoyed tying flies badly for half a
lifetime. And while I understand many of the reasons people don't tie, I do have a complicated reaction to somebody saying, "I would, but I'm no good at it."

Neither is Sophie, who one week past her third birthday tied her first fly. Of course, I plan to have her study under Ken Hanley's daughter, Sierra, so seven years from

229

now I expect my daughter shall sit in judgment of poor Dad. By then she'll be keener than a Gamakatsu point, but kindly, tolerant, fond; she will smile, watching me at my vise talking to myself and dribbling bits of material which stick fast to my feet of clay.

"Dad," she'll say sweetly, "you really do get a kick out of that, don't you?"

Right. Not bloody likely, if she's anything like I was at ten, when I took myself and my activities seriously, competing with a vengeance—a "Nike" child, in today's lexicon, for whom only first place counted. Winning was not actually a source of satisfaction, but the only way to avoid scathing self-recriminations attending any loss. Whenever my father, a fierce competitor of another sort—he'd flown fifty missions over North Africa—would suggest "It's only a game," I dismissed him; clearly he had no grasp.

By thirteen I was much worse—miserable, absurd. Any firsts that year were subsumed by the agonies of a second in judo, a third in archery, and an all-star selection woefully flawed because it wasn't *unanimous*. Then between sets of tennis my father started dying, and while I held his hand waiting for the ambulance I exchanged something of my driven childhood for this revelation: The First Thing Is To Live.

My father did, that time. Things changed. For the better? For the worse?

It might take much of a life to address that rightly. I don't think there's anything obvious about the evolution of the answer. Perfectionism has its place, and if your ambition is to own Rhode Island you'd better not let up a bit or acknowledge that anything less than everything is enough; it's also best that you not recognize that you're going to die pretty soon—and that when you do, Rhode Island won't float after you into the ether.

On the other hand . . . a glimpse of mortality can be very instructive. It often prods a person to refine his vision of what's important. "Rhode Island or nothing" might still be the result, but it's common that a person enlightened by a look at the Dark begins to see the value in what previously seemed little things: friends, family, tiny wild trout. Perhaps even doing something for the pure pleasure of it, like tying a fly an expert would disdain but a fish might eat. When that happens, you can think, "I'm so clever, by my own lights," and not let the dependent clause get you down.

None of which means that you don't try to get better or strive for excellence. I just took a class to nudge myself forward: I've now stood duck-quill wings on a fly—one on each side, too—so I can forever refuse to do that again while feeling smug that I could. I've also folded Humpies so neatly they do not resemble the fibrous droppings of rodents; and Larry Flynt might admire the proportions of my A.P. Nymph, even if Andy Puyans himself was only cooing out of kindness.

I will never be a master, I know, for lack of little things: patience, fine motor control, the desire to split hairs and details. But I should let that stop me?

God forbid, because I'm also not the best caster, cook, writer, or lover. (Hang on, I'm going upstairs to check on "lover" again.)

Practice. You've got to want to do it. Because you like to. Because the process is a pleasure, which can only be true if you forgive a few trespasses, unless that means letting thread crowd the head. I study fly tying and fish my homework. In public and print I am modest, humble, knowing of place. Privately I credit myself with developing an entirely original technique about every other month—not merely a unique pattern, you understand, but an approach never even attempted by the hand of man.

By the hand of *this* man, it always turns out: a great advantage of ignorance is that it provides opportunities to imagine you've done something special, with vast implications for the wider world. (Yonder lies Vanity; that way there be danger.) So far I've always been wrong, or rightly the new master of a non-viable procedure. Still, I almost always get a week of mild thrill, and usually a batch of flies I can fish with.

Sometimes not. Take, for example, the not-patented Norman Cello-Sandwich Vein-Wing (not to be confused with the Norman Single-Taped Vein-Wing, which is soon to be the most famous fly ever developed near the Walgreen's at High Street not far from Macarthur). Please note that this technique resembles one found in *Caddis Superhatches*.

1. Tack two feet of clear, wide packing tape sticky side up along the edge of your workbench.
2. Clean a bunch of deer hair somewhat longer than you want your wing, then seize the butt ends with small, strong, clothes-pin style wood clamp, causing the hair to flare widely.
3. Lay flared-hair wedge on tape perpendicular to length. Repeat steps 1, 2, 3 along the length of the tape.
4. Coat the entire (now hairy) tape with contact cement, and then lay a second piece of tape on top of first, thereby cello-sandwiching the flared-hair wedges. Allow to dry overnight.
5. Cut out wedges, trim to shape and tie in to patterns in place of hair. (Use flat for stonefly adults, for example, or fold to create caddis tent wings.)
6. Admire finished fly profusely. Look at from beneath, the trout's perspective, expressing amazement at how lifelike these wings appear.

7. Test by dropping into a large bowl of water.
8. Watch as it sinks like a stone. Swear, say, "Woe is Me!" Admit failure and start over. If you're of a literary bent, and alone at the time, quote John Waller Hills, from *River Keeper:* "Angling is an endless quest in which no one ever attains perfection, and we stumble towards it not by conquests but by defeats."

Sophie may already understand Hills's insight, though her first fly was anything but a failure. The thing certainly came as such a surprise—at least to me.

It's true that since infancy Sophie has often sat on my lap while I tied. I'd usually get one fly out of this arrangement, then we'd whip one up for her. Sophie favors bright, contrasting colors of marabou and long sweeps of flashy feathers and fibers, although I'm not aware of Atlantic salmon or steelhead sorts in the family woodpile.

The way the system works is that I'll hold materials in place as she winds the bobbin in circles. These circles do tend to get larger and larger, however, until at last a single rotation around the now-distant hook shank becomes a dynamic windmill motion involving considerable effort and not a little peril. But eventually she says "Tie it up, Daddy," and I finish for her, clip the hook at the bend, then pass the cut edge across a grinder or file. The remainder is a fly "fixed" in the fashion of male cats, to which I tie a light cord, making for Soph a necklace she wears with great pleasure for eight or ten minutes.

The other day, it was different.

I'd set up a pair of vises on the dining-room table, as preparation for showing a young would-be fly fisher the one thing—not two—I know about spinning deer hair. As we were waiting, Sophie said, "I want to tie a fly."

I did the "Well-all-right-but just for a minute, come sit on Daddy's lap" routine.

"No, Daddy. I want to tie my *own* fly."

Whoa.

"You just put the string on the hook for me."

I obeyed. Sophie held the bobbin in one hand in a fashion suggesting resistance was futile. With the other she rummaged through the materials I'd brought up—a disappointing lot, by comparison with the chaos of treasures littering my desk downstairs.

She found a loose grizzly hackle and tied it in. By the base, curved side forward. "How did you remember how to do that?" I demanded, but she had no time for idle chatter. Incredibly, I saw that while concentrating she had clenched her teeth on the tip of her tongue—like me, like my father, and like Michael Jordon, though his technique is pretty sloppy.

Sophie tied on another hackle, this one brown.

"That's so good, Soph."

"Daddy?"

"What?"

"Daddy, I'm busy."

She actually said that. *Then she palmered the hackle.*

Here let be it known that I have no interest in creating a prodigy of any kind, that it was I who argued that we should cut her off from *Sesame Street* when she started counting to ten at twelve months of age. Now here she is, still seven inches shorter than my best trout, palmering a fly that might catch him.

She makes a mess of it. That's a relief.

She realizes she's messed up, starts over, does a better job and ties the stem down, matting the barbs a little by winding backwards. She wraps forward the other hackle, adds two peacock herls and a strand of lime green

Flashabou. Finally, with the sharp scissors she's not usually allowed to use, she trims it all down to a shape she likes.

"Okay Daddy tie it up. Now another one."

Sophie ties three altogether. I carefully lavish praise, if that's possible. But I'm also waiting for her to show some sign of pride, as she does after finishing a pirouette, or half a somersault, or when we do the Funky Chicken all the way down.

She seems rather . . . matter of fact.

"Here, Daddy. These are for you."

"Why, thank you. They're just wonderful."

Sophie looks at the flies, then at me. Her expression is still . . . *sober,* shall we say, and for a moment her gaze un-focussed. She can't be comparing her efforts to an image of what she wanted, can she? At last she gives me one nod, then says evenly, "Fish with them, Daddy."

That is the idea, or part of it. As for the rest . . . I figure I've got seven years before she's shrewd enough to assess Daddy's crockery. Long before that, though, I hope to teach her some perspective, skipping the coronary lesson, if I may.

25

❧❦❧

Satrap of Sunfish

❧❦❧

The Carson swirls about my knees and I am unbalanced a little, not by tailwater current, but by an image of a corpse my friend found here last spring.

He had partners that day, two police officers on vacation, who soberly agreed that they'd never seen a body so badly decayed. The local sheriff concurred. About the lost man's identity, or cause of death, nobody had a clue.

Now it's summer. Morning sunlight scatters across the riffle where my Wulff begins to drag. A hundred feet above me a truck courses the highway along the high canyon wall.

Fall? Push? Did the man winter over in this deep water? Or did he sleep on some Sierra slope, rushing down with snow-melt to tumble the runs, float sluggishly through pools. . . .

The nymphs crawl in, the nymphs crawl out. I can't believe that would-be mayflies bothered him much. Caddis worms? Golden stones? God, *dobsonfly nymphs*, hell-grammites, with a score of spiky gills-that-walk, and black, blind-looking heads, mandibles like pruning shears. . . .

I shudder, roll-cast, dry the fly, present. I know there are fish here, good fish, but I've seen none.

I'd done better the evening before, fishing a warmwater pond outside Auburn, hunting bass from my float tube. Only two took a popper, but I hung, briefly, bluegills in numbers that increased by the hour. Curiously enough, the more I caught the closer to me I caught them; soon I couldn't dap my rod without hooking up.

I imagined that I profited from failing light, but no; while landing a fish I looked down to discover myself the featured attraction for an excited bluegill horde. Each time my fins fanned debris from the weeds a dozen of these darted forward to snatch out particles from the pale cloud—and my popper when I dropped it. If I held still they slowly backed away, suspending at rod's reach to watch me intently.

I felt silly. In my own mind I might be "Master of Meander," but to these small subjects I was something else altogether. Duke of Detritus? Satrap of Sunfish? A maelstrom force bringing bounty and taking sacrifices for a minute or two. . . .

I don't remember pondering this, that morning on the Carson. Not until I quit casting to change flies. Then I caught a flicker of movement in my peripheral vision and found, holding just behind my leg, a trout as long as my forearm. *Right there*, a foot behind my knee, keeping tight to the seam I created in current and sheltering in my shadow, the best trout of the season. *Then* I remembered the bluegill to whom I'd served dinner. *Now* I was trout habitat.

It's important to define yourself for yourself, obviously enough; obviously others define you in terms specific to their need. Roles—we are fathers and sons, providers, enemies and friends, part of a herd on the freeway. As a fly fisherman I step lightly, seek cover, stalk. I work for the natural drift, to seduce with size and shape and color. In a niche of mind I consider myself an elegant predator, refined from ancestors killing for food into a creature whose ethics verge on Quixotic. Still, I am of the wild world, I hope: so if for this fish I am a rock, an island, good cover—why not?

Angling is usually too engrossing to divert attention to such wayward streams. But there do come moments when I discover an unexpected fit in a scheme: breaker of current or creator of same, caster of shadow or stirrer of silt. If this is so in life. . . .

Somewhere the lenses from my father's eyes see the world for another; perhaps they are still filled with the wonder he felt. In me today cells replicate codes my father passed on. Parted out, carrying on, deliberately or accidentally, we relay gifts in a vast organic race. And sometime last year a man fed the Carson with flesh prey to processes more ancient than awful.

Trout and bluegills and carnivorous nymphs cannot contemplate meaning. I can, in a morning when I am matter still mostly composed. And since it's fishing which tempted me to thoughts of "Desiderata," then it's fair enough that as fisher I feel more at ease. In my time I will wander, seeking my station in places of water and woods; this sustains my spirit. Beyond life, shorn of craft and free of artifice, my flesh will join others: why not with creatures of river? Worse fates, I think, than to nurture at last a fine trout like the one who finds me an island.

But that's then. Right now I am an angler and have life's work before me. Arrested in sunlight, steady in current, I struggle with a question much more immediate, full of drama and desire—

—how the hell can I dead-drift a fly past my knee?